THOSE ANCIENT DRAMAS
CALLED TRAGEDIES

I. Reconstruction of the Ancient Theater at Athens

THOSE ANCIENT
DRAMAS
CALLED TRAGEDIES

BY

William Kelly Prentice

NEW YORK / RUSSELL & RUSSELL

To
Maria Prentice
this book is affectionately
dedicated.

CONTENTS

ILLUSTRATIONS

I

RECONSTRUCTION OF THE ANCIENT THEATER AT ATHENS. *Frontispiece*

This is a reconstruction by August Frickenhaus of the theater at Athens as completed under Lycurgus, treasurer of the city in the third quarter of the fourth century B.C. It was published in *Schriften der Wissenschaftlichen Gesellschaft in Strassburg*, Heft 31, 1917, Tafel II. Probably much of this theater was constructed before the end of the classical period. This reconstruction is open to criticism. For example, objection may be made to the colonnades in the inner angles of the projecting wings of the stage-building, and to the large base for an altar before the central door. But it is possible to imagine the performance of the classical Greek dramas in a setting very similar to this.

II

RUINS OF THE ANCIENT THEATER AT EPIDAURUS.   *Facing page* 11

This theater was built towards the end of the fourth century B.C., about a century after the first productions of the tragedies of Aeschylus, Sophocles, and Euripides. It was much smaller than the great theater of Athens, for Epidaurus was a small town which in the classical age was more important as a health resort than as a city. But this is the best preserved of all the Greek theaters older than the Hellenistic period. The photograph is reproduced here from Margarete Bieber, *The History of the Greek and Roman Theater*, Princeton University Press, 1939.

I

THE ORIGIN OF "TRAGEDY"

THE word tragedy did not suggest, originally, death or sorrow. To the ancient Greeks *tragos* meant goat and *aoide* meant song. Thus *tragoidia* ought to mean the singing of the goats, and most scholars believe that this word was applied first to choruses of men who, at certain festivals, dressed up like goats and danced and sang to please a god, known to the Greeks in the earliest times by various local names and later on called commonly Dionysus.

It is often said that Dionysus was the god of wine. But that is a very misleading statement. The Greeks believed that this god was one of those supernatural powers which, in some mysterious way, have to do with reproduction. He was the god who, in the springtime, made the sap flow again in the dry boles of the trees and in the roots of all the plants, so that these send forth again stalk and blade, leaf and flower, fruit and grain, on which the lives of animals and of men depend. And as each year this god reawakened nature and created anew the vegetation of the earth, so also he caused the animals to bear offspring and reproduce their species. Thus it seemed that he was the cause of the continual existence of all life, and to some extent of all civilization, prosperity and happiness. Moreover, as it was believed that it was this god who raised from the dead the plants which seemed to die each year, leaving their roots or their seeds buried in the cheerless dark, so it was believed that he had something to do with that resurrection of men after death in which the ancient Greeks believed, however vague and uncertain their conceptions of such a resurrection were. Lastly, it was thought that this god had power over the minds and dispositions of men. Wine was associated with him only because this liquid, more than any other known to them, seemed to these Greeks to have in it something of the mysterious, invigorating power attributed to this god. So also the fauns, satyrs, and other imaginary creatures of the wold were associated with him and, among the common animals, the goats, because all these seemed especially to partake of his exuberant nature and quickening vitality.

A primitive people, living directly from the products of their fields and livestock, might well consider such a god most necessary to them. Without him there would be no crops, no increase of the flocks and herds: all life would be extinguished. To attract the attention of their god, to obtain his presence and his aid, primitive peoples have often engaged in performances which they believed to be pleasing to him. Sometimes they have dressed up as, and imitated the actions of, creatures with which, as they imagined, their god loved to consort. That is why primitive Greeks, on certain occasions near the turning of the year, dressed up as goats, satyrs or silenuses, and danced and sang to win the favor of their god of reproduction.

All peoples, everywhere, seem to take pleasure in dressing up, in acting a part. The taste and talent for dramatization seem to have been stronger in the ancient Greeks than in most other peoples. Thus it happened that very early among these Greeks the performances of mummers dancing and singing for Dionysus began to develop into what we know as the Greek drama. The song of the chorus began to tell a story with a connected plot, doubtless at first some story about Dionysus. Perhaps impersonation entered into the performance first when someone dressed up as the god himself and appeared in person to listen to the song. Perhaps then the impersonator of the god sometimes discussed the story with the leader of the chorus, elaborating the story by supplying details which the chorus supposedly did not know, and thus a beginning was made of dramatic dialogue. Presently other persons involved in the story were introduced and

these, instead of merely telling the story, actually reproduced certain scenes in dialogue and action. Then stories
other than those directly concerning the god himself were
chosen for presentation in this way and, at least in the
tragedies, the chorus ceased to represent the imaginary
animal-like associates of the god, and appeared in human
form as the subordinate associates of the principal character
in each story — citizens or soldiers, councilors, women or
maidens. By this time the scenes reproduced by the actors,
which at first were interludes in the narrative of the chorus,
had become the chief means of unfolding the story, while
the dancing and singing of the chorus, once the essential part
of the performance, had become mere interludes in the action.
Finally the choruses were omitted altogether.

Some of these early Greek dramas had a more serious tone
than others, because of the different conceptions of the god
in his various cults. In some of these cults Dionysus was
identified with the spirit of plant life collectively, and, as
many of the plants seem to die each winter and to return to
the earth from which they sprang, emerging again each year
as if reborn in the sunlight, warmth, and beauty of the
springtime, so the legends of these cults told of the sufferings as well as of the joys of Dionysus. The alternation of
sorrow and joy, which was characteristic of these legends,
was regarded as typical of the vicissitudes inherent in all life.
Hence in these cults the presentation of any suffering or of
any reversal of fortune seemed appropriate to the festivals of
this god. In these cults the choruses which performed at the
festivals seem originally to have dressed up as goats, and
for this reason their performance was called tragoidia. When
the goat costume was abandoned and the chorus appeared
as the human associates of the principal person in the story,
the performance really lost its original and essential character altogether. But the original name for such performances

in these cults, tragedy, i.e. the song of the goat chorus, was retained. When the plots for tragedies ceased to be taken exclusively from the legends of Dionysus himself, with rare exceptions they were taken from the traditional legends of other gods, or of the heroes of the olden time. Apparently this was a convention, due to the essentially religious origin of the Greek drama, which few were willing to ignore. But these legends furnished only the barest outlines of a story. The situation presented in each, which was the basis of each dramatic plot, was in most cases typical of a kind of situation which might arise in the life of any of the audience at the play, or in the life of any of us now: it might be, and often was, treated as an allegory. Moreover, most of the episodes, the personalities of those involved, and all the dialogues were freely created by the ancient dramatist himself, and all the ideas developed in the course of the play were his. Thus several plays, very different in the personalities of the characters, in the episodes, and in the intellectual or moral implications, were sometimes written by different dramatists from the same legend.

Greek tragedies are not always sad. Sometimes they involve no tragedy in the modern sense at all; sometimes they end happily. But always they are serious in tone; always they contain some moving crisis, and appeal strongly to the sympathy, feeling, and reason of thoughtful people, so that Aristotle (*Poetics* VI, 2) could define tragedy as a form of drama "effecting through the exercise of pity and fear the purgation (catharsis) of such emotions."

In Aristotle's definition of tragedy pity and fear seem to be selected as typical of the emotions to be purged. There is no difference between pity and fear in Aristotle's treatise, except that the one is aroused by the contemplation of some distressing thing which has already occurred, the other by the expectation of some distressing thing which has not yet

occurred. A person who watches when an accident is about
to happen experiences fear up to the moment when the accident does occur: in that instant all fear disappears and the
observer feels pity for the sufferers. But Aristotle can not
mean that it is the function of tragedy to rid people of
emotions such as pity and fear. He must mean cleansing whatever organs or mechanisms produce the emotions, and so
increasing the flow of the emotions. That it is uplifting and
pleasurable to have our emotions roused and stimulated is
known to everybody. Even fear is sought by children and
adults, and it is enjoyed if the person frightened is not scared
too much. If the chief function of tragedy is to rouse and
stimulate the emotions of the audience, the Greek tragedies
fulfill this function admirably.

Tragedies at Athens in the fifth century B.C. were presented in groups of four, of which the first three were of
this developed type, while the fourth, a shorter piece called a
satyr-play, retained a good deal of the original character of
"tragedy." The first three plays in each group were called,
together, a trilogy. All four together were called a tetralogy.
Sometimes the three plays of a trilogy dealt with parts of one
connected story, so that while each play had a plot of its own,
yet there was a plot underlying all three together, uniting
them as a whole like the acts of a modern drama or opera.
We have one example of such a trilogy still extant in the
Oresteia of Aeschylus, consisting of the *Agamemnon,* the
Choephori and the *Eumenides.* This is the only extant trilogy.
In some cases, however, the plays of a trilogy seem to have
been entirely unconnected. To Athenian tragedies of the fifth
century B.C. exclusive of satyr-plays, this book is devoted.

In other cults of Dionysus the god was regarded as the
ultimate source of all reproductivity, especially in animals
and in man. Hence, in the performances of choruses at the
festivals of these cults and in the dramas which grew out

[7]

of them, the virility of the god was emphasized, as well as his power to quicken animals and men to reproduce their kind. Such performances often, even characteristically, involved much that seems to us sensual and lascivious. In them, originally, the chorus did not appear as goats, but as imaginary, lecherous creatures like Silenus, and their performance was called comedy, from the Greek word *komos,* a merrymaking or a band of revelers. Later, when the primitive character of the early performances had been outgrown, the choruses were composed of imaginary, often quite fantastic figures, as in the *Clouds* of Aristophanes. Much of the primitive sensuality was refined away, but much of the ribaldry and facetiousness was retained, as well as the name comedy. Commonly, however, the plots of the comedies were free creations of the authors, without dependence upon the traditional, sacred legends. Many of the characters and situations were taken from everyday life, and in their more serious parts the comedies of Aristophanes and his contemporaries dealt with political and other questions of their times.

Early in the fourth century both tragedy of the kind produced by Aeschylus, Sophocles, and Euripides, and comedy of the kind written by Aristophanes, had practically come to an end, and in the second half of that century both were replaced by what is known as the "new comedy" of Menander and others. This so-called new comedy was far more a development of the tragedy of Euripides than of the old comedy of Aristophanes. It lacked the obscenity and scurrility characteristic of the "old comedy." It also lacked the "parabasis," an interlude in which the chorus spoke directly to the audience, discussing some political, social or literary topic without affecting the plot or action of the play. Like the tragedies of Euripides the new comedies had articulated plots, each presenting throughout a consistent story. On the other hand, the plots of the new comedy as of the old were freely invented

[8]

by the authors, and were not based even formally on ancient legends. The episodes, although often exaggerated, reflected or parodied scenes in the daily life of members of the audience themselves. The characters were human persons, of types familiar to all — the young lover, the beautiful slave girl, the dissipated rake, the churlish father, the smart, unscrupulous servant, the moneylender, the procurer, the doddering old man, the truculent soldier. The choral performances became mere interludes without vital connection with the action, and were ultimately omitted altogether. Moreover, these plays seem uniformly to have lacked any moments of high emotional tension or appeals to reflection: they were designed solely to entertain and amuse the audience.

This new comedy of the Greeks was the chief source of the Roman comedy of Plautus and Terence, and this in turn had the greatest influence upon the development of the European drama since the renaissance, including the Elizabethan drama and our own.

The Greek drama, both tragedy and comedy, then, originated in the performances of choruses which danced and sang to attract a god and to secure his assistance. Such performances needed besides the performers and their costumes only a fairly smooth and level surface such as many open market places or threshing floors could furnish without any special preparation. At first the audience doubtless simply stood in a ring about the performers, as the audience still does at many folk dances in modern Greek villages. As the performances became more complicated and the crowds of spectators increased, it became necessary to construct dancing floors at the foot of hills, on the slopes of which the spectators could sit in tiers. Such a dancing floor, used for choral or dramatic performances was called by the Greeks an orchestra: it was level, and commonly circular. Later on a building was erected on or tangent to that part of the orchestra which was farthest from the spectators. In the fifth century B.C. this building was of one story, perhaps with a second story over its central part; it served as a background for the scenes, it reflected the voices of the speakers and the music towards the audience, and it furnished what we would call the stage-setting for the plays, representing a temple, a palace or a group of dwellings, from which some of the actors could enter the orchestra and into which exits could be made. In its interior it also provided dressing rooms for the performers. At the same time, seats for the spectators were constructed on the hillsides, first of wood and afterwards of stone. Such a theater naturally took the form of a cockle-shell with its sides rising steeply against the hill, enclosing the circular orchestra on three sides, and having the "stage-building" along its straight edge. Between the ends of the auditorium and the stage-building passages were left, through which, before the play began, the spectators could reach their seats and, after the play began, entrances to and exits from the orchestra could be made. There was no stage, at least through most of the fifth century, actors and chorus alike appearing on the ground level, either in the orchestra or immediately in front of the stage-building, and often mingling with each other; there were some advantages in that. Later on, most if not all of the orchestra was occupied by spectators, and consequently the performers appeared on a raised stage. The whole theater was open to the sky. Some of the ancient Greek theaters were very large. The great theater at Athens held about fifteen thousand people, the last seat being about three hundred feet from the front of the stage-building and about a hundred feet above the ground level. The orchestra in the fifth century had a diameter of a little more than seventy-eight feet: in the fourth century this orchestra was about sixty-four feet in diameter and its auditorium had seventy-eight rows of seats.

II. Ruins of the Ancient Theater at Epidaurus

Some memories of the ancient Greek theaters are preserved in our own. For example, the central part of the auditorium, which is more or less level and commonly has the form of a horseshoe, is still called the orchestra, as well as the band of musicians who are seated in front of the stage; boxes for spectators at each end of the auditorium proper are still called proscenium boxes, the ancient proscenium being the space immediately before the stage-building. In certain important respects, however, modern theaters are very different from the ancient ones. In ancient Greek theaters there was and could be no curtain: consequently, there could be no great change in the stage-setting after the play began, although in a few plays, as for example in the *Choephori* and in the *Eumenides* of Aeschylus, some change in the locus of the scenes is made and indicated in various ingenious ways. In most cases all the action, even intimate conversations, took place in the open before the stage-building, and whatever was supposed to take place elsewhere had to be described by some actor. Furthermore, all the entrances and exits of the performers, including the chorus, had to be accounted for in some plausible way, and at the end some equally plausible way had to be devised in which the performers then present could be withdrawn. This is not so in our modern stage.

Brander Matthews, in his *Principles of Playmaking*, (Charles Scribner's Sons, 1919, p. 89) said: "In the Attic theater the performers stood in the orchestra which curved into the hillside of the acropolis; in Shakspere's theater, as in Molière's, certain spectators were accommodated with seats on the stage itself; and in the theaters for which Beaumarchais and Sheridan composed their comedies the stage jutted out far into the house, so that the actors actually turned their backs on a certain proportion of the audience. But in the final quarter of the nineteenth century this platform-stage gave way to the picture-frame stage to which we are accustomed in our snug modern theaters; and nowadays the actor is not in close proximity to the spectators; he is not surrounded by them on three sides; he is withdrawn behind a picture-frame; and he is bidden not to get out of the picture."

It is worthy of recognition that the ancient tragedians, without a curtain or stage machinery or stage lighting, and without much scenery except a fixed background, could produce dramas which so profoundly affect the thoughts and emotions of all men.

II

THE *PROMETHEUS BOUND* OF AESCHYLUS

I T is not always possible to determine the contents of the ancient legends from which the ancient Greek tragedians constructed their plots, because in the ancient mythological books, such as the so-called *Bibliotheca* of Apollodorus which seems to belong to the first century after Christ, and likewise in most modern books on mythology such as Bullfinch's *Age of Fable*, the ancient myths are boiled up together with the stories created out of the bones of these myths by the dramatists and other poets. Thus it is often assumed that the story of Prometheus presented by Aeschylus in his *Prometheus Bound*, or the story of Agememnon's return in Aeschylus's *Agamemnon*, is identical with the legend already familiar to Aeschylus and his audience. That is not the case. The *Prometheus Bound* is based on two legends, one of Prometheus and one of Io, artificially combined by Aeschylus. The version of the Prometheus legend selected by Aeschylus was that Prometheus, a Titan or son of a Titan and a brother of Atlas, saved the human race from the destruction planned for it by Zeus, brought fire from the gods to men and showed men how to use it, and taught men all the arts of civilization which make man's life endurable: therefore Zeus in anger caused Prometheus to be fastened to a cliff on the remotest border of the earth — apparently somewhere in the farthest northeast — where his body was torn continually by an eagle or a vulture; but Prometheus, being an immortal, did not die in his suffering and was ultimately released and restored. The legend of Io selected by Aeschylus was that Io, a beautiful maiden and perhaps priestess of Hera the consort of Zeus, was beloved by Zeus; when this intrigue was discovered, Io was changed into a heifer — she was associated in some way with the moon, and this association suggested the horns and the metamorphosis — either by Zeus to conceal his relations with her, or by Hera to prevent this intercourse. Hera then made the giant Argos the guardian of the heifer; but Zeus sent Hermes to kill Argos. After this, Hera sent a monstrous gadfly to torment the heifer, so that it was driven to wander distracted through all the world. Finally, Io was restored to human form and bore to Zeus a son, who was sometimes called Epaphos, and who became the ancestor of many.

The plot of the *Prometheus Bound* is as follows. Hephaestus with his attendants, Might and Force, drag in the rebel Prometheus, and, at the command of the reluctant and somewhat sympathetic Hephaestus, these attendants fasten Prometheus to the rock. When his tormentors have left, the chorus, consisting of the daughters of Oceanus, appears in a winged car, from which later on they descend into the orchestra. In a long dialogue with the chorus, which genuinely sympathizes with him, Prometheus tells of his services to Zeus and to the human race, and of the causes of the wrath of Zeus against him. Presently Oceanus himself appears, riding on some sort of four-legged winged creature. Oceanus claims to be Prometheus's friend, asks how he can help him and, when his profession of friendship is treated with contempt, advises Prometheus to submit to Zeus. When Oceanus withdraws, the chorus sings an ode expressing its sorrow for the sufferings of Prometheus. In reply Prometheus, in a friendly but mournful tone, continues his account of his services to mankind. This is followed by another ode of sorrow. Then Io appears with horns but apparently otherwise in human form. In a long dialogue between Io, Prometheus and the chorus the whole story of Io is told, including all her wanderings and sufferings, both those which have occurred already and those which are still to come. It is made to appear that both she and Prometheus are victims of the ruthless cruelty of an immoral god. Io says that she does not see how she can ever escape from her misery; but Prometheus tells her that deliverance

will come for both, that his deliverer will be a descendant of
Io herself, and that Zeus will be dethroned. When Io withdraws, Prometheus talks further with the chorus about the
fall of Zeus which he predicts, and expresses his contempt for
Zeus and for all the agony which he foresees for himself.
Hereupon Hermes enters, appearing as a servile messenger
from Zeus. He is truculent. He first warns Prometheus, then
arrogantly demands that he tell plainly the secret which threatens the power of Zeus, and finally he threatens Prometheus
with still greater torments. Prometheus is undismayed, and
Hermes, after warning the chorus to retire lest they be involved in the punishment of Prometheus, withdraws. Immediately, amid thunder, lightning and whirlwind, the whole
cliff with Prometheus upon it sinks into the ground.

It hardly seems as if anything could have been left unsaid
or unthought about the *Prometheus* of Aeschylus in all these
centuries. And yet, in considering the problems which such a
drama undoubtedly presents, our minds are often beclouded
by inherited traditions and prejudices concerning the ancient
Greeks and their literature. We know that some of these traditions originated long ago in very dull and narrow minds;
but we still preserve them by a kind of perverted scholarship.
It may be that with respect to the *Prometheus* we have all been
influenced, more or less unconsciously, by such traditions and
prejudices. Moreover, it is certainly a mistake to attempt to
synthesize, as many scholars are prone to do, all that the ancient Greeks have said on any subject, or even to interpret
every saying of an ancient author by what the same author
has said elsewhere. For example, it may be that the conception
of Zeus presented in the *Prometheus* is fundamentally different from the conception of Zeus in the *Agamemnon*. It is also
a dangerous practice to interpret ancient literature as if it
were modern. The danger lies in our natural tendency to

project upon ancient times thoughts and feelings which are natural and common now, but which were alien to the ancient world, thereby ignoring the ideas and beliefs of the ancients which we have outgrown. On the other hand, it is equally dangerous to assume that the ancients thought and felt otherwise than we, especially if we hold, as we do, that among the ancient Greeks were some of the ablest minds which the human race has produced. This assumption would stretch every utterance of an ancient thinker upon the Procrustean bed of our traditional conception of the ancient world, and at the outset beg the question in the prosecution of any nonconformist.

There is an idea, which is present in much of our modern thinking on matters of religion, that, as the human race advances, the religious views of the more enlightened and spiritually minded tend to become increasingly remote from those more primitive notions embodied in a traditional literature and mythology, or in the creed and ritual prescribed by an organized priesthood, and preserved essentially unchanged by the religious conservatism and superstition of the masses. This may seem to some an essentially modern idea and foreign to the ancient world. But it is certain, at least, that contemporaries of Aeschylus were convinced that the conceptions of the gods involved in their traditional literature and in popular belief were irreconcilable with what gods must be, if there are gods at all. It seems clear to me that Aeschylus also held this view. I do not mean merely that an interesting comparison may be drawn between the religious ideas of Aeschylus and our own: I mean that certain religious ideas similar to ours were consciously held by Aeschylus, and were deliberately incorporated by him in this drama. If this is so, then we may properly seek to interpret this drama in accordance with these ideas.

The common interpretation of the *Prometheus* is that the poet took certain well known myths, and with his artistic genius gave to them dramatic form. If these familiar stories are all this drama contains, there is no reason why anyone might not understand it completely, and doubtless this is all it did contain for the mass of Aeschylus's audience. These stories are presented in scenes which involve much that is theatrical or spectacular, amounting sometimes to what we should expect in a modern melodrama. How the audience must have enjoyed seeing Might and Force drag in the struggling Prometheus and pinion him to the cliff, while the reluctant Hephaestus stands by! How they must have wondered at the sea maidens arriving in their winged car, or at old Oceanus with his dragon! How the horned Io and the account of her wanderings must have interested them! How they must have been thrilled by the awful cataclysm at the end! What might seem to us ridiculous in these spectacles was not so for those who believed that these supernatural beings really existed, and who were familiar from childhood with stories of such occurrences. Theatrical effects seem characteristic of Aeschylus's plays, and are the chief reason for their notorious popularity. Processions and spectacular scenes crowd the stage in the *Oresteia* and the *Seven Against Thebes*. These were plays which everyone, however unintelligent, could and did enjoy. And when we remember the extreme beauty of its verses, the sublime fortitude of its hero, and the pathos with which the innocent and pitiful Io is presented, we need not wonder at the success of the *Prometheus*.

But surely this is not all that the *Prometheus* contains. Justly it has been called the most profoundly moving drama of all literature. Profundity is not specially involved in the legends selected, and it cannot be by accident that through his presentation of these legends the poet awakens in us the deepest thoughts concerning the existence and nature of divinity.

[19]

That Aeschylus produced a play suited to the comprehension of a crowd is evident. That the same play had a deeper meaning for the more thoughtful in his audience is also possible. Some modern scholars, seeking such a deeper meaning, see in this, as in many other Greek tragedies, human character exhibited on a supernatural scale. Prickard, for example, sees in Prometheus a mythological figure like Oedipus, in which a human character struggling under overwhelming injustice and suffering is presented to view. But neither Prometheus nor Io is an obviously human type: the human traits they display are incidental rather than essential to this drama. Others hold that Prometheus is the uncompromising champion of liberty, crushed in the conflict with autocracy, ultimately to arise triumphant. But Prometheus in this drama is the benefactor of the human race, not a champion in any sense: Io is the innocent victim of a ruthless tyranny.

There is, however, another interpretation of this drama, which is at least more plausible. To many Prometheus is the heroic sinner, the rebel against the divine order of things-as-they-are, to which all should conform. Such persons hold that the essence of morality for the ancient Greeks was conformity to the transcendent rhythm of the universe, of which each individual is an integral part. From this point of view it was right and necessary that Prometheus should be "rhythmized," that is, reduced, by torments if need be, to conformity. Thus they hold that Prometheus was for the Greeks a typically "tragic" figure, involved by fate and circumstance in the hopeless antithesis of two resistless forces, in this case the passion for liberty and the duty of conformity. For us the balance is unequal and our sympathies are wholly with Prometheus, only because conformity to an organization of the universe which included the traditional Greek gods has ceased to be the ultimate morality.

But this explanation is not complete, not wholly satisfactory. It fails to account for certain features of this drama which constantly recur, forcing themselves upon our attention. Why, for example, is the statement so often reiterated that the gods against whom Prometheus rebelled are *new* and *transient,* even though themselves contrasted with ephemeral men? Or why are these gods, with the possible exception of Hephaestus, represented throughout as so extremely and repulsively anthropomorphic, wanton, and vile? Why are these two legends in which the gods appear at their very worst united here, although there is nothing in the traditional mythology which associated Io directly with Prometheus? Why is it that, although Oceanus, Io, Hermes, and even the sea maidens urge Prometheus to submit and conform, their pleas are made so weak and unconvincing? They must have seemed unconvincing even to the ancient Greeks as we commonly imagine them. How is it, finally, that the last scenes of the play glorify Prometheus's uncompromising resistance on the ground that the existing authority will be ultimately dethroned or transformed?

Of course Prometheus was a mythological figure well known to all of Aeschylus's audience. And perhaps this was all he was to most. He is presented here in form more or less human, and with human characteristics. How else could he have been presented on the Greek stage? Even such abstractions as Might and Force are presented here in human form. But like many other mythological figures, Prometheus, as his name implies, is also a personification thinly veiled in the myth. Primarily it is the mythological figure which Aeschylus took as his hero, and conforming with the practice of the Greek tragedians he introduces into his drama nothing which is contradictory to the accepted legends. Within the bounds of this convention, however, the myths and mythological figures are made the vehicles of his thought.

Prometheus belonged to the ages of Uranus and of Cronus, as well as to this present age of Zeus. This drama does not explain how Uranus was overthrown, but we are told how the fall of Cronus came about. When the Titans undertook to defend Cronus, Prometheus offered his services to them: their strength and his intelligence united would have sufficed perhaps to maintain the older order. But the Titans would have none of him: they chose to rely on force alone. Hence Prometheus, knowing that force without intelligence could not succeed against deceit, joined Zeus, a willing ally to a willing lord: Zeus the deceitful, guided by intelligence, was better than blind force. By the intelligence of Prometheus Zeus was enabled to overthrow Cronus and all the old régime of heaven, making himself supreme. By reason of the power thus acquired through Prometheus's aid Zeus assigned to each of the lesser gods his special rights and functions. Yet later in the play Prometheus says that this also was done by him and not by Zeus: "Who else but me did make complete assignment to these new gods of all their several functions?" Once enthroned, this Zeus became autocratic, violent and ruthless: he neglected, then sought to destroy utterly, the present human race. But Prometheus withstood him for the love he bore to man. He gave men hopes — blind hopes, it is true, but hopes that freed them from too anxious a presage of an ultimate doom. He taught men all they know. Unthinking brutes before, he made them advance step by step through all the stages of their civilization. He gave them fire and taught its use, thereby making possible all those activities which depend on its employment. In short, as he says himself, "all arts to mortals from Prometheus come." Thus by Prometheus, and by him alone, there was provided for the race of men life which was comparable, in some respects at least, to that of the gods themselves.

Because he withstood Zeus and befriended man, Prometheus incurred the enmity of this new ruler of the universe, and therefore he was transfixed and pinioned upon the lonely crag at the uttermost limits of the world. Yet he foresaw that unless he, the prisoner, saved the tyrant, the tyrant himself would in time be overthrown in consequence of some act which he would perpetrate unless he was deterred. What that act would be is not fully explained: only it would be a marriage, one more last sexual anthropomorphic union among the gods. But this deliverance of Zeus would not be effected unless Prometheus was delivered from these bonds. His release would not be by the hand of Zeus. The liberator who would release Prometheus would be one born of woman, descendant of Epaphos, the son of Io, whom Zeus would engender, not sexually, but by touch alone. Therefore Prometheus, though he suffered, would not submit to the tyranny of this upstart ruler whom he himself had once enthroned. He knew that this ruler could not wholly destroy him, not though he heaped more torments, tenfold more, upon his helpless head, and compassed the ruin of the earth and the sky in the outpourings of his wrath. Twice already Prometheus had seen such rulers of the universe swept from their seats of power. He would yet live to see the present tyrants in their turn dethroned if they would not submit themselves to his guidance and restraint. The time would come when he would be released from bondage, and then, if fate willed it, would this Zeus turn once more to seek his love, and league with him, as eager as he would be eager for this new alliance.

What can this Prometheus be but Reasoning, foreseeing Intelligence, which alone bestows on gods and men alike their powers and their prerogatives? There even seems to be a clear hint of this interpretation in the opening scene of the play, where Cratus says to Prometheus: "Falsely the gods call thee Intelligence: thou thyself dost need intelligence to get thee clear of this skilful work of ours." But this Intelligence may be enthralled and oppressed by the very gods whom he has himself enthroned, and then some one of the race of men must needs release him.

Who are these gods, these new and transient gods, who appear in this strange drama? They are so vile! It was inherent in the legends of Prometheus and of Io that the gods involved therein should appear like men; but surely their anthropomorphism is here unnecessarily emphasized by Aeschylus. It seems as if the poet had tried in every way to make the gods appear as evil as possible. Not much is said about the other gods, but Zeus at least is vividly portrayed. He is arbitrary, irresponsible, violent, lustful, cruel, and ruthless. He is a tyrant. Yet we feel that he is a type of all the rest. Hera is lightly touched upon, but appears to be as human and cruel as her spouse. Hermes is truculent, servile, and ridiculous. Hephaestus alone appears reluctant to execute the cruel orders of his master. But all alike are enemies of Prometheus and equally hated by him. They are hostile to the human race. Nearly the whole play is devoted to the display of the vindictive cruelty of these gods to Prometheus, whose only fault was that he befriended man, and to Io, whose only fault was that she was lovely.

Are these the gods in whom Aeschylus believed? That he was a deeply religious man, and believed that gods really existed, is evident from his other dramas. But the Zeus of the *Prometheus* is very different from that mighty, inscrutable deity of whom the chorus in the *Agamemnon* sings, who rules the world with justice, and who, though he has set this law to be supreme for men that "understanding comes by suffering," has done this to promote righteousness in men, and not in wanton cruelty. The gods of the *Prometheus* are the gods of the traditional Greek mythology. They are not eternal. There have been other gods before them, and they themselves in turn will pass away. Real gods, if there be real gods, do not change; but men's conceptions of them change. The conceptions of the gods presented in the *Prometheus* are those which the Greeks of Aeschylus's time had inherited from a cruder and less spiritual age, embodied in their myths and sacred literature, and developed by the imaginations of their poets and artists into characters as repulsive to the thoughtful Greeks of the fifth century before Christ as they are to us. Such gods as these are gods created by man in his own image, and by him exalted until they enchain and torture the intelligence by which they were created, terrorize and disgust their creators. The intelligence by which they were created will survive them. But man alone can liberate the intelligence by which they may be reconstructed in accordance with man's own intellectual and spiritual development. For such gods have no objective reality : they exist only in men's minds.

This play of Aeschylus is complete in itself. It matters little whether or not it was one of a trilogy treating a single subject, like the several chapters of a book. We know little, practically nothing, of the other plays which are commonly grouped with this. We do not know with certainty that they were grouped together by their author. It is not necessary that we should. The problem with which Aeschylus was dealing in this extant play is definitely presented to us.

The same problem arises for every group of men who, having advanced beyond a more primitive stage of their development, seek to hold fast religious conceptions inherited from an earlier period, because these are incorporated in a literature which they consider sacred, and because all are reluctant to abandon or reconstruct their religious beliefs. The same problem faces the world today, and for the same reasons. We should not wonder, then, that Aeschylus in his time dealt with this problem in veiled language, and so cautiously that many in all these intervening centuries have failed to recognize, or at least to agree upon, his deeper meaning.

Those who speak out plainly on such subjects are often held in great dishonor, and are thought by many to be doing incalculable harm. Such protestants have arisen in all ages; there are many of them now. But little good will come of all their argument until the time is ripe. Till then the wise speak with caution and try not to defeat their purpose by extreme statements which might destroy beliefs which many hold most dear, and which many would be unable to reconstruct or to replace.

Parts of the foregoing Chapter are reprinted from THE CLASSICAL WEEKLY, XV, 1921, pp. 26-29.

III

THE *AGAMEMNON* OF AESCHYLUS

T HE date of the *Prometheus Bound* is not known. Probably it was written when Aeschylus was growing old. It is possible but not certain that it was performed on the same day as *Prometheus the Fire-Bringer* and *Prometheus Released,* and constituted a trilogy with these dramas, both of which have been lost. It is quite certain that it was earlier than the trilogy called the *Oresteia,* which was performed in 458 B.C., for soon after this Aeschylus went to Sicily on his second, or perhaps his third visit, and died there in the year 456-5.

The *Oresteia* is the only trilogy of all the Greek tragedies which has been preserved to us complete. It consists of the *Agamemnon,* the *Choephori* and the *Eumenides.*

The legend on which the *Agamemnon* was based was very familiar to the audience. In the form adopted by Aeschylus, Agamemnon was the king of Argos and overlord of all the other Greek princes. His wife, Clytemnestra, was the sister of that Helen, the wife of Agamemnon's brother Menelaus, who was stolen by Paris. To recover Helen, Agamemnon collected a host, which assembled at Aulis in Boeotia, each contingent under its own chieftain or leaders. But adverse winds continually prevented the fleet from sailing. Consequently, to assuage the winds, Calchas, a prophet, persuaded Agamemnon to sacrifice his oldest daughter, Iphigenia. The fleet then sailed and the Greek host besieged Troy for ten years. Ultimately Troy was captured, sacked and burned. But meanwhile Clytemnestra fell in love with Agamemnon's cousin Aegisthus, and with him planned to kill Agamemnon on his return. Throughout the last year of the war the conspirators kept a watchman on the east coast of the Argolid, to signal by a beacon on the mountain top to another watchman on the palace roof the approach of the conqueror.

Evidently the real purpose of this arrangement was not known to the people of Argos. Warned in time by the beacon the conspirators were able to carry out their plan; the veterans with Agamemnon and those in Argos who were loyal to him were overawed. Agamemnon was killed by Clytemnestra herself when he was preparing for a bath, and Clytemnestra with Aegisthus reigned in his stead. See the introduction by A. W. Verrall to his edition of the *Agamemnon,* second edition, 1904.

The plot of Aeschylus's *Agamemnon* is as follows: The play opens with the appearance of the watchman on the roof of the palace. It is still night, but immediately before the dawn. The watchman sees the beacon and reports to Clytemnestra. The elders, or senators of Argos, who constitute the chorus, are summoned to the palace, before which a crowd has already collected, doubtless including partisans of the conspirators with arms concealed under their cloaks. The elders discuss the origin of the war, a war ordained by Zeus on account of a "woman of many husbands," which has brought calamities on Greeks and Trojans alike. They ask the reason for the celebration which is already in progress, and for their summons to the palace. They then continue their reflections on the war, dwelling on the sacrifice of Iphigenia, and asserting that they find no explanation for all these horrors except in the will of Zeus who guides men to wisdom, establishing as his ordinance that *understanding comes by suffering.* Then Clytemnestra appears from the palace and announces to the assemblage that the beacon which has just been seen is the last of a series of signal fires, lighted on high points all the way from Troy. The distances, according to Verrall, are "for the first two stages about sixty miles, for the third stage about a hundred miles": there were eight stages in all. The queen then tells that these signal fires have conveyed the news that Troy has been taken at last, pictures the situation in the captured city and in the Greek camp, and says that the victors may now be expected home soon.

When she withdraws, some people, either the chorus as most of the editors suppose, or some of the bystanders, profess gratitude; but from what the elders say a little later, it is evident that they at least, though astonished, are not convinced by the queen's story, even if they feel unable to contradict her. To the audience, if they knew already that the beacon really meant that Agamemnon with the remnant of his fleet was about to arrive home, the whole account of the chain of signal fires must have seemed a deliberate falsification on Clytemnestra's part. In the choral ode which follows after her return to the palace the elders sing of the wrath of the gods for the sins of men, particularly the sin of Paris and Helen, and for the arrogance and cruelty of princes who abuse their power. At the end they suggest that there is indignation in Greece itself against the conquerors, and that retribution is imminent.

Immediately after this a herald from Agamemnon appears, announcing that the fleet has arrived at the harbor. He tells of the victory, of the destruction of Troy, and of the punishment of the city and of Paris for the rape of Helen. The chorus, in conversation, hints that the situation at home is far from satisfactory. The herald says that all has ended well: he describes the hardships of the army during the long siege, but says that for those who have survived all sufferings are now over and that great glory has been won. Clytemnestra appears again for a moment, claims that her interpretation of the beacon has now been justified convincingly, asserts her loyalty to Agamemnon, and protests that she has always been a faithful wife. When she withdraws again, the herald in answer to questions from the chorus says that, as far as he knows, Menelaus is still alive, but that his ships disappeared in the storm which has just occurred.

He describes the storm at some length and then retires. The chorus then sings of the coming of Helen to Troy and the consequences. The ode ends in a contrast of arrogance with righteousness. Then Agamemnon appears with the veterans of the Trojan war and with Cassandra, the youngest and fairest of the daughters of Priam, assigned to the conqueror as his special prize: they are escorted to the square before the palace by soldiers of Argos, evidently acting on orders from Aegisthus and Clytemnestra. The chorus welcomes the king, who replies in a dignified, though somewhat austere speech to the populace. The queen reappears with attendants carrying a crimson carpet. In a long, unctuous speech she professes love for Agamemnon, expatiates on what she describes as her grief during his absence and her anxiety for his safety, and explains that their child, Orestes, is not at home because she has sent him to Phocis lest he be killed by revolutionists while the king was away.

At her command the attendants lay down the carpet from the doorway to his chariot, and she invites him to walk this path of red (i.e. of blood). He answers with some asperity, but at last consents, telling her, however, to be kind to the princess, now his slave, whom he has brought with him. As he passes her she exclaims that it is as coolness in the summertime when a man perfected (i.e. his life completed) passes to his home (i.e. the grave), and when he enters the door, she, turning back, prays: "Oh, Zeus, Zeus, the fulfiller, fulfill my prayers, and may it be thy will to accomplish that which thou wilt do." Clytemnestra herself then enters the palace, the carpet is removed, and the chorus sings an ode full of foreboding. The queen comes out again, and not unkindly tells Cassandra to follow her into the palace. But Cassandra makes no answer to her, and Clytemnestra leaves her angrily. There follows a long and highly dramatic dialogue between the chorus and Cassandra.

Cassandra, the princess, was also a prophetess. Beloved of Apollo, the god of prophecy, she promised, then refused, to yield her body to the god. For that a curse was laid upon her that her prophecies would never be believed. Now, at first in a sort of frenzy, incoherently, later calmly and plainly, she reveals her knowledge of the past and of the future. She knows that this palace is hated by the gods and is defiled by atrocious murders by members of the family of the slain. She knows the story of Thyestes' children whom Atreus, his brother and Agamemnon's father, slew, and whose bodies were served to their father to eat. She seems actually to see before her eyes these children bemoaning their own butchery. She seems to see Clytemnestra, the wife, about to kill her husband Agamemnon. She foretells the immediate death of Agamemnon and of herself. But she prophesies that one now in exile (i.e. Orestes) will come to slay his mother and avenge his father, adding: "I will go in and meet my fate: I will endure to die: I greet this portal as the gate of Hades." Then, with great dignity and sadness she enters the palace alone.

Soon afterwards the groans of Agamemnon are heard, and the elders press forward to enter the palace. But they hesitate and discuss what to do. Doubtless, as Verrall suggests, partisans of the conspirators, who were standing quietly near the entrance, have now moved across the passage, preventing any attempt to rescue the king.

Soon Clytemnestra appears and boasts that she has killed her husband with her own hand. She asserts that she was justified, because he had sacrificed their daughter, had been unfaithful to his wife by consorting with many captives in the camp at Troy, and had crowned his other atrocities by bringing the captured princess to his very home. She announces that Cassandra also has been killed, and proclaims herself the righteous avenger of the sins of the house of Atreus. The elders are outraged and indignantly threaten

her with retribution; but she warns them that she has now
the mastery and will force all who resist her to submit.
Aegisthus then appears for the first time, accompanied by
soldiers. He tells in detail the story of the killing of his
brothers and the expulsion of himself by Atreus, boasts
that it was he who planned the death of Agamemnon, and
threatens the elders with imprisonment and starvation. After
some angry debate, Aegisthus is restrained by Clytemnestra
who says that enough has been done. Aegisthus and Clytemnestra then retire into the palace, the chorus, i.e. the elders,
march away, probably under guard, and the crowd disappears.

In a theater without a curtain it is necessary to provide an
adequate reason for the entrance and the exit of every person
who appears in the play. Sometimes this is difficult, especially
at the beginning of a play and at the end. In the modern
theater this difficulty does not exist: if the author so chooses
the curtain may rise on a scene in which many persons are
already present, and at the end the curtain may fall suddenly
on a scene in which the whole cast is participating. In the
ancient Greek theater every single person connected in any
way with the performance must enter and leave in full view
of the audience: when the play begins the orchestra must be
empty, and when the play is over all those present at the last
must leave in some apparently natural way. Moreover, an
ancient Greek play, as far as entrances and exits are concerned, normally consists of one single act.

The *Agamemnon* of Aeschylus opens with the appearance of a watchman on the roof of the palace of the Atreidae.
Evidently he has been lying down on the roof. He could have
climbed there through a trap door before the play com-
menced, unseen by the audience, and could have lain there
concealed by the parapet. When it is time, he rises, yawns,

stretches, walks up and down in plain sight. So the play begins. It was done this way at the Harvard performance in 1906.

At the conclusion of the play the elders, i.e. the chorus, are led away, probably by a guard of soldiers. Clytemnestra and Aegisthus retire into the palace. The bodies of Agamemnon and Cassandra — if they have been brought out — are taken back into the palace and all the other people in the orchestra drift off to their customary occupations, or else all those left in the orchestra form a funeral procession and escort the bodies to burial. Thus the orchestra is made empty again and the play ends.

In the first episode Clytemnestra tells the chorus (which represents the councilors of Argos) that the beacon which the watchman has seen and reported signifies that Troy has been captured on this very night just past. The queen withdraws, the chorus sings, and then, immediately, a herald appears announcing that Agamemnon and the victorious Argives have already arrived at their own shore. Consequently, it was supposed by everyone until recently that the Athenian audience was expected to imagine that an interval of perhaps two weeks had elapsed between the first and the second episodes of the play. But no audience could imagine such a lapse of time while the same persons — chorus, populace, soldiers and servants — remained in the same places before their eyes. If these persons withdrew from the orchestra and after a short pause reappeared, there is nothing in the play which accounts for their reappearance. If these persons remained in the orchestra, inactive for a moment to suggest a lapse of time, it would be impossible to account for their continued presence during the suggested interval. Verrall in his Introduction has given the true explanation. The beacon did not relay a message from Troy: it was a signal given by watchers posted by the conspirators to give them warning, and it signified that the fleet was sighted and that Agamemnon would be home in a few hours. That was in the legend as the Athenians knew it. Therefore the Athenian audience knew from the beginning that Clytemnestra's story of the fire post was a lie, intended to delay action on the part of those who were loyal to the king. The chorus in the play did not know that. They evidently did not believe the story, though they could not be sure that it was false, and they seem not in the least surprised when, a few moments afterwards, the herald appears. The later Greeks, however, accepted Clytemnestra's speech at its face value, and thoughtlessly included it in the genuine tradition. The only reason I can discover or imagine for rejecting Verrall's explanation is a passionate desire to believe in the historicity of the fire post.

Clytemnestra's deliberate and elaborate falsehood must have made a very bad impression on the audience. Moreover, there was great danger that a wife who conspired with her lover to kill her husband and to seize his throne, who actually killed her husband with her own hand, would seem such a monster that all sympathy for her would be lost, so that the drama would have less effect upon the emotions of the audience. Consequently, in the early part of the play Aeschylus takes great pains to present the faults of Agamemnon as strongly as possible. Agamemnon appears cold and ruthless, obsessed by his own grandeur. His cruelty to his daughter, Iphigenia, and to the conquered Trojans, the miseries which he had brought upon Greeks and Trojans alike, his neglect of his own kingdom and his wife, the arrogance of the manner in which he brought the captive princess to his home — all these things are emphasized. Thus some balance of sympathy for both the principal characters is preserved, and the horror and emotional effect of the play is enhanced.

After Agamemnon has entered the palace to meet his death, there follows a scene in which Cassandra recalls the horrible events which have already occurred, pictures the miseries of her own life, and then foretells the brutal killing of Agamemnon which is about to take place and her own violent death which is to follow immediately. At times she seems in a frenzy, her speech sometimes incoherent, her cries delirious. To one who only reads the play and does not see it on the stage, the scene seems long and perhaps tedious. But if it were well acted it would have a most powerful effect on any audience. Apart from its intrinsic pathos, however, this scene has certain particular functions in this play.

1. It presents, vividly and emotionally, the horrors of the past, and thus creates a mood of horror and suspense.

2. It presents, in all its ruthless brutality, the Trojan war — in a sense Cassandra is the incarnation of the misery caused by war — and thus, by enhancing the condemnation of Agamemnon, it tends to justify Clytemnestra to some extent.

3. By reminding the audience of the details of the story which the audience already knew, e.g. the injuries done to each other by the two brothers Atreus and Thyestes, and especially the killing of Thyestes' children and the serving of these children's flesh as food to their own father, by describing the killing of Agamemnon by his wife Clytemnestra, which is about to take place, and by foretelling the return of Orestes in the more distant future to kill his own mother, this scene shows the murder of Agamemnon in relation to its horrible antecedents and consequences.

4. The prophecy of this murder, at the very moment when it is about to take place, presents it to the imagination rather than to the sight of the audience, and yet so vividly that it makes unnecessary the showing of the murder on the stage,

although, to a modern dramatist, this would seem unquestionably a *scène à faire*. In our modern theater much is sacrificed for the sake of intense excitement, whereas these ancient Greeks seem to have believed that excitement tends to paralyze the reason and dull the finer emotions, and hence they avoided scenes of physical violence.

5. Finally, the spectacle of the princess Cassandra, fully conscious that a violent death awaits her, but with immense courage, dignity, and sadness, entering alone that door through which Agamemnon has already passed, is one of the most moving spectacles imaginable.

When Cassandra also has entered the palace, the chorus sings an ode, very short but long enough to suggest the passing of a time sufficient for her to be killed or to be removed to some inner room. Then the outcries of the dying king are heard. Immediately the elders start to go to his rescue. But they do not go. Instead of that they stand there and debate with each other on what they should do, each speaking two verses. To one who reads the play this debate at first sight seems intolerably absurd. But if, at the performance of the play, there were a good many persons present under orders from the conspirators, if these persons showed that they were armed, and moved forward between the elders and the palace door, then the debate would not seem ridiculous at all. These old men could not force their way into the palace against an armed resistance.

When Agamemnon and Cassandra are both dead, Clytemnestra reappears, and, in speeches to the chorus and the bystanders, though she speaks as if she thought she was justifying herself, she reveals her wounded vanity, her hatred for Agamemnon, her jealousy of Cassandra, her love for Aegisthus. She makes it apparent that these passions supplied the real motive for her acts of violence, not a desire to avenge the death of Iphigenia. Thus, at the end of the play she stands condemned. But she is not the only one at fault. Agamemnon is condemned also. The audience is left with the impression that all these horrors were due to the wanton selfishness, lust and cruelty of certain individuals, Agamemnon and Clytemnestra in chief.

IV

THE *CHOEPHORI* OF AESCHYLUS

THE second play of the trilogy called the *Oresteia* is the *Choephori*, i.e. the *Libation Bearers*, which takes its name from its chorus composed of maidens, attendants of Electra, who carry libations to the tomb of Agamemnon. The legend on which it is based is that Orestes, son of Agamemnon and Clytemnestra, during his father's absence at Troy and his mother's intrigue with Aegisthus at home, was sent to Strophius, king of Phocis in central Greece, whose wife was perhaps a sister of Agamemnon and so the boy's aunt. Orestes may be supposed to have been about ten years old at that time. In Phocis he formed with Strophius's son Pylades a friendship which has become proverbial. When Agamemnon and Cassandra had been killed by Clytemnestra, and Aegisthus was reigning in Mycenae (or in Argos, according to the version adopted by Aeschylus), and when Orestes had grown to manhood, he, in obedience to an oracle which conveyed to him a direct command from Zeus, returned to his home with Pylades his friend, was reunited to his sister Electra, killed both Aegisthus and his own mother Clytemnestra, and became king in his father's place.

The plot of the *Choephori* is as follows. At dawn Orestes and Pylades come to the grave of Agamemnon, and Orestes leaves upon it two locks of his own hair. A company of women is seen approaching, and the two young men conceal themselves behind some sort of screen. These women are the princess Electra and her attendants; they have been sent by Clytemnestra to pour libations on the tomb and thus to appease the spirit of the dead king. The choral ode with which they enter, and the conversation between the chorus-leader and the princess make this clear. The women discuss how they can make the offering to appease the spirit of Agamemnon when they wish his spirit to assist in wreaking vengeance on Clytemnestra and Aegisthus, and what sort of a prayer they can make. When they have agreed about these things, Electra describes the present situation and her own condition, "no better than a slave's," and, invoking Hermes, the spirits of the underworld, and in particular the spirit of her father, prays that Orestes may come home, that an avenger may appear, and that those who killed her father may in return be punished with death. She then pours the libations and in so doing discovers the locks of Orestes' hair. Orestes and Pylades reveal themselves, and Electra is at length convinced that one of them is really her brother. Orestes appeals to Zeus, and to Apollo who gave the oracle, and asserts the justice of the attempt which he is about to make to avenge his father's death.

A long scene follows in which, in a dialogue sung to music as in a modern opera and highly emotional, the brother and sister, encouraged by the chorus, nerve themselves to kill their mother. It must have been clear to the audience, and it is felt by modern readers of the play, that it was tremendously difficult for these young people to obey what they believed to be a divine command in doing what they must have believed to be fundamentally wrong. There have been many instances in actual life in which men, for religious or other reasons, have felt obliged to do what was immoral or contrary to natural affection. At the same time, it is also clear that Orestes and Electra condemn the behavior of Clytemnestra and Aegisthus, especially in the killing of Agamemnon, and that they are bitterly indignant on account of what they themselves have suffered. Orestes has been robbed of his home and of the kingdom; Electra has been denied her rights as the eldest princess of the house, and has been treated as an inferior. They have brooded for years over the injustice done to their own selves. Thus they have nursed a grievance of their own, which tends to balance their natural obligation to their mother. Thus they seem more human; the acts of violence they contemplate ap-

pear less unnatural. Finally Orestes makes a plan, and assigns
to each one his part. Electra and her attendants are to return
to the palace, keeping secret the arrival of the prince. Orestes
himself and Pylades are to present themselves as travelers
bringing a message that Orestes is dead, and thus they are to
obtain admission to the palace and an opportunity to kill
Aegisthus and Clytemnestra.

The next scene is before the palace. Electra and her attendants appear, the princess entering the palace alone, the chorus
remaining outside. Then the two young men arrive, call for
the doorkeeper, and ask to see the masters of the house. The
porter takes their message and goes within. Clytemnestra
comes out and receives the strangers courteously. Orestes tells
the story he has concocted, and Clytemnestra directs a servant
to show them to a guestchamber. All then withdraw into the
palace except the chorus and perhaps certain bystanders, while
the chorus sings a short ode.

A woman-servant from the palace now appears, sent out by
Clytemnestra to call Aegisthus, who is absent somewhere, to
come at once with guards. The chorus asks her to summon
Aegisthus without telling him to bring a guard. She does so.
The chorus sings a rather long ode, to give time for the servant to find Aegisthus and for him to reach the palace. Aegisthus arrives, seeks out the strangers in the guestroom, and is
killed by Orestes there. Hearing the commotion, Clytemnestra
rushes out, learns what has happened, and calls for a battle-
axe as if she had the intention of fighting it out herself: she
understands that one of the killers is her own son. Orestes and
Pylades come out, and Clytemnestra begs her son to spare his
mother. Orestes hesitates, but Pylades, speaking now for the
first time in the play, reminds him of the oracle. Clytemnestra
still pleads for her life; but Orestes, now relentless, forces her
indoors and kills her in the guestroom beside her husband's

body. Thus both the killings take place off stage, in accordance with a convention of the Greek drama.

Presently, after another choral ode, Orestes reappears, the bodies of the dead are brought out, and with them the robe in which Agamemnon was entangled when he was killed. He justifies his actions, pointing to the bodies and to the robe with which his father was entrapped, and announces that he will now go as a suppliant to Apollo's shrine, evidently to be purified from the stain of shedding kindred blood — to Greek minds one of the most heinous sins. The chorus approves what he has done. But at that moment he seems to see the Furies already in pursuit of him. Doubtless the Furies were not visible to any in the orchestra or in the audience; but Orestes, in a frenzy, rushes off followed by Pylades. The bodies and the robe are removed, and all the attendants, the chorus and the bystanders retire. Electra has not reappeared at all. Thus the orchestra is left empty again.

In the *Choephori* the action takes place at two different localities, the grave of Agamemnon and the palace. Evidently the grave is thought to be at some distance from the palace and not visible from the palace door. Yet because of the lack of a curtain and of modern scenery both grave and palace must be in full view of the audience, continuously, from the beginning of the play to the end. How could that have been managed in a Greek theater?

To the grave, which must have been somewhere in the orchestra, Orestes and Pylades come, very early in the morning, to make an offering there before they begin the attempt to carry out their mission. That is a natural and plausible beginning for the play. Since they come from a distance and by land, they enter the orchestra, in accordance with the conventions of the Athenian theater, through the entrance on the left of the audience. Perhaps before the play began something had been brought into the orchestra which would suggest a grave, and perhaps also something which would suggest shrubbery behind which these young men could conceal themselves. These things must have been placed well forward in the orchestra, in order not to interfere with the action in other parts of the play, and must have been well over toward the left of the orchestra from the spectators' point of view. The procession of Electra and her maids then comes out of the palace, turns to its left (thus turning the backs of the women to the grave), leaves the orchestra by the passage on the right of the spectators, passes around the back of the stage-building and, after a suitable interval, reenters the orchestra through the passage on the left of the spectators through which Orestes and Pylades had come. Later, when all leave the grave for the palace, all go by the route followed by the women but in the opposite direction, leaving the orchestra on the spectators' left and entering again on the spectators' right, thus creating the illusion that the way between the palace and the grave does not lie across the orchestra, and that the grave and the palace are distant from each other.

The evidences by which the brother and sister recognize one another are not very convincing, and the recognition scene in Sophocles' *Electra* is undeniably better. However, it may be thought that there was something distinctive about the hair of Agamemnon's children — it may have been red or unusually golden — perhaps one can imagine also that there was something distinctive about the shape of their footprints. In any case, the means of identification are not really very important.

After the recognition follows a long scene at the grave where the tyranny of Clytemnestra and Aegisthus is made plain, arousing the indignation of the audience and sympathy for Orestes and Electra, and the spirit of Agamemnon is invoked to aid his children in the almost impossible task before them. The scene seems to us too long and tedious. But it should be remembered that it was necessary for Orestes and Electra to steel themselves, not only to incur great danger, but also to kill their own mother in cold blood. The very length and tediousness of this scene seems to me to show that Aeschylus felt it necessary to emphasize the horror of what Orestes proposed to do, and to show that Orestes and Electra were fully conscious of this horror, but accepted its necessity.

Throughout the whole play Pylades is present with Orestes constantly, but he speaks only once and then very briefly. Orestes addresses some remarks to him, but these could have been made in soliloquy. But when, at the most critical moment, Orestes hesitates to kill his mother, then Pylades reminds him of the oracle. Pylades is carried along through the whole play in order to make this one speech of three verses only. But this speech is ultimately the deciding factor: it shows that, as Aeschylus presents the story, Orestes killed his mother in obedience to an explicit command of God.

At the end of the play it is not necessary to assume that Orestes really saw the Furies, or that they were really visible to anyone. Orestes *seems* to see them and rushes out, followed by Pylades.

V

THE *EUMENIDES* OF AESCHYLUS

THE third play of this trilogy is called the *Eumenides,* i.e. *The Kindly Ones,* a name given later in plays by Sophocles and Euripides to the Furies or Erinyes, that is, the Avengers. It is not known exactly on which legend Aeschylus based the play. Much of the play was apparently invented by the author. There was a legend that Orestes was purified by Apollo of the sin of killing his mother, but that the Furies refused to recognize the purification, and continued to pursue and torment Orestes, until he was absolved by bringing to the territory of Athens, probably to the town of Brauron, a statue of the goddess Artemis from the land of the barbarous Tauroi, or in some other way. There was also a legend among the Athenians that their ancient court, called the Court of the Areopagus, was first established to try Orestes for killing his mother, and that, when the trial ended in a tie vote, Athena herself gave the casting vote which exonerated Orestes.

The plot of the *Eumenides* is this. At dawn a priestess appears and, in a long soliloquy, makes it clear that the stage-building is to be considered the temple of Apollo at Delphi. She gives a history of the cult and of the oracle there. Then she enters the temple, but returns immediately in terror : she has seen within a suppliant, with bloody hands and sword, and before the man, asleep on benches, the Furies, whose appearance she describes. Presently Orestes comes out of the temple with Apollo himself. The god says that he will not abandon him, and calls Hermes, his brother, who appears from somewhere, to conduct Orestes to the shrine of Pallas Athena on the Acropolis of Athens. Hermes and Orestes leave through the passage at the left of the audience, and Apollo apparently returns into his temple. What becomes of the priestess is not clear : she does not speak again, and probably she is so fright-

ened that either immediately or a little later she flees from
the place through the passage on the spectators' right. Then
the ghost of Clytemnestra appears somehow in the orchestra.
She wakens the Furies, who are heard moaning and whimper-
ing like sleeping dogs inside the temple; when they are
roused the ghost disappears.

The Furies, who constitute the chorus of the play, now
come crowding out of the temple, bemoaning the fact that
while they slept their quarry has escaped. They complain that
Apollo himself, the son of Zeus, has stolen away a man who
killed his own mother. Such are the doings of these "newer"
gods, whose power exceeds justice. Ancient justice required
that an act, such as the shedding of kindred blood, should be
punished irrespective of its cause or motive. It is the right and
the obligation of the Furies to enforce this ancient justice.
Apollo comes out of the temple again and orders them off. He
says they are hated by all the gods. They taunt him with full
responsibility for the killing of Clytemnestra, because he commanded Orestes to commit the act and afterwards protected
him. He charges them with inconsistency, because they did
not pursue Clytemnestra who killed her husband. They reply
that a wife is not of the kindred of her husband, and assert
that they will never abandon the pursuit of Orestes. Then, like
a pack of hounds, they pick up the scent and disappear through
the passage on the left, while Apollo withdraws into the
temple. Thus the orchestra is entirely emptied. Evidently there
are no bystanders.

The next scene has a different location. Orestes appears
from the passage on the right, and shows by his first words
that the stage-building is now to be considered the temple of
Athena at Athens. He enters the temple and disappears. The
chorus of the Furies then comes in, following Orestes' track.
They look in through the temple door and see him clasping
the statue of the goddess; Athena herself is absent. Orestes

comes out, asserts his purification by Apollo, and claims the protection of Athena, wherever she may be. The chorus, in a very long choral ode, asserts that the Furies are the enforcers of strict justice, that their function is to punish, that their power to do so is irresistible and inalienable, that the gods have no control over them. They exult in anticipation of the vengeance which they expect to take. Athena now returns from afar. She first questions the Furies, and then turns to Orestes, who tells his story and submits his case to her decision. But she says that to decide a case involving, as this one does, "manslaughter of a kind which (prima facie) would call for immediate wrath and judgment" is not allowed even to her. Orestes has come to her purified from the pollution of his act. The Furies, however, have a claim not easily dismissed. Therefore, she will now go to select the best of her citizens, i.e. of Athens, and establish a court for the trial of such cases. She then leaves for the city through the passage on the right (which in the Athenian theater did actually lead to the city). While she is gone the chorus sings another ode: they resent the submission of this case to any authority or any court. The case is clear as it stands. An act of killing within the ties of blood-kindred has been committed, circumstance or motive is of no importance. Theirs is the duty to enforce this ancient law of retaliation. It means the destruction of all the ancient order and security by new ordinances, if the plea of this matricide is to prevail.

Hereupon a procession enters from the right, i.e. from the city, including Athena, a herald, the jury of the Areopagites, and a crowd of other citizens. The court is formed somewhere in the orchestra, at a little distance from the temple, just as the hill called the Areopagus lay a short distance in front of and in plain view of the Acropolis. Apollo appears as the chief witness and counsel for the defense. The chorus of Furies as prosecutor examines the defendant, who admits the facts of the killing. Apollo pleads the cause of his client and debates with the chorus. Both are angry, and the arguments on both sides are specious and unconvincing. Incidentally, Apollo remarks that when once a man is killed there is no restitution: "For this my father has provided no remedy, though all else he has disposed according to his will." Athena charges the jury, and the jurymen then cast their ballots. Evidently the balloting takes some little time, during which there is further acrimonious conversation between Apollo and the Furies. When the balloting is over, Athena announces that in case of a tie she, as presiding officer of the court, will give the casting vote in favor of the defendant. The votes are counted and prove to be equally divided; Athena announces that the defendant is acquitted. Apollo then withdraws. Orestes, with dignity and emotion, expresses his gratitude to Athena and to the Athenians for his deliverance, and promises perpetual friendship between his country (Argos) and Athens. Then he also withdraws.

When Orestes has gone, there follows a very curious dialogue between the chorus and Athena, the chorus at first singing to music bitter and passionate words, Athena speaking quietly and calmly. Twice, in exactly the same language, the chorus cries shame on these newer gods who have ridden down the ancient laws, say that they, the Avengers, have been dishonored, assert their implacable hatred and destructive anger. Twice Athena answers them that they have not been dishonored, that Zeus himself has willed it that Orestes should be absolved; she pleads with them not to be vindictive, not to visit Athens with calamities, and promises to them honors, and worship, and greater happiness both for themselves and for the people. Twice again, in exactly the same language, they express their rage and assert that trickery of the gods, "hard to struggle with," has robbed them of their prerogatives. Twice again Athena answers them, patiently

and mildly, for they are older than she and (should be) wiser;
but she still speaks firmly, urging them to lay aside their anger
and, "bestowing good, receiving good, in goodly honor, to
have a portion in this most god-beloved land." Then suddenly
there is a complete change in the Furies, a change which does
not seem to have been caused by anything which Athena has
said, but which may have been accounted for in the acting
of the scene, as Verrall suggests. Something may have suggested the direct, though probably invisible, intervention of
Zeus himself. Athena herself expresses gratitude to Persuasion, who directed her appeal, but says that it was Zeus,
the guardian of assemblies, who prevailed. Mildly now, first
in simple speech and then again singing, the chorus asks about
the honors assured to them by Athena, accepts "a home
wherein to dwell with Pallas," promise their favor and vow
eternal peace and happiness for Athens and the Athenians.
Thereupon, by the command of Athena, the Furies, escorted
by the court and all the bystanders, march away through the
passage on the right to their new abode. Athena doubtless returns to her temple, and the orchestra is left empty.

In the *Eumenides* also there are changes of location, but
here the changes present no serious difficulties. The play has
three parts. It opens at dawn with the appearance of a priestess
coming from the city with a temple key. That shows that the
stage-building is now supposed to be a temple. The first words
of this priestess show that this is the temple of Apollo at
Delphi, but as a whole the rather long soliloquy of the
priestess seems to me an artificial and unmotivated declamation, detracting somewhat from natural realism: perhaps it did
not seem so to the original audience. What is said and done by
those who appear next confirm the identification. At the end
of the first part of the play everyone then present leaves the
orchestra, doubtless passing out at the left of the audience,

and when they appear again, at the right of the audience, the spoken lines show that the stage-building is now to be regarded as the temple of Athena at Athens. In neither case is any object before the temple necessary for the identification of the building. In the second part of the play there is no statue of Athena visible. In the first part the priestess, having entered the temple and come out again, describes what she has seen within, Orestes at the omphalos, the Furies asleep (on the benches?). In the second part, Orestes from without the temple addresses Athena as if she were within. Later, the Furies, looking in at the temple door, tell what they see inside, namely Orestes before the statue there, which the audience cannot see. Later still Athena herself appears outside of the temple, having come, as she says, from the Scamander. At no time is anything inside either temple visible to the audience.

When the priestess has reappeared from the temple of Apollo, Apollo himself comes out with Orestes, and sends Orestes to Athens with Hermes. Apollo addresses Hermes, but it is not necessary to suppose that Hermes is visible. Orestes leaves by the passage on the left of the audience, to appear later on the right of the audience. It is not clear to me whether Apollo reenters the temple or leaves the orchestra by one of the passages as if he were going somewhere else, or remains somewhere at the back of the orchestra where he will not interfere with the ghost of Clytemnestra. A trial performance of the play would show which procedure is the most effective. The ghost appears, doubtless through a trap door over a tunnel under the orchestra. The ghost goes to the door of the temple and from there, without entering, wakes the sleeping Furies. When the ghost disappears—perhaps by the way by which she came, or perhaps around the end of the building — the Furies come out. They act a good deal like a pack of hounds, especially when they whimper in their sleep within the temple — the sounds being heard through the open door — and when they pick up the scent of the fugitive and leave the orchestra. Whether they attempt to re-enter the temple and are prevented by Apollo is uncertain; again a trial performance would show the best way. Perhaps this question depends on the significance of the word ἔξω, used by Apollo in addressing them. Finally the Furies run off after Orestes; Apollo leaves, probably on his way to Athens also. Probably the priestess has remained outside all this time, crouching against the front of the temple or hiding behind a column, if there were columns there then. Perhaps she re-enters the temple now to perform her usual duties there, and doubtless she now had some extra house cleaning to do; perhaps in her fright she runs away towards the city. Thus the orchestra is empty again. I suppose that none of the ordinary citizens are abroad yet.

The trial scene and all that happens after Orestes with-draws take place in the open space before the temple of Athens, i.e. in the orchestra. The conversion of the Furies is probably correctly imagined by Verrall. The final scene, when all those present escort the Erinyes, now become Eumenides, to their new sanctuary, could be made very spectacular. Perhaps even Athena and Apollo join the pro-cession, adding to the splendor of the spectacle.

There is much in the extant plays of Aeschylus that is spectacular in the commonest sense. Perhaps it was this quality more than any other which made his plays popular among most of his audiences.

VI

THE TRILOGY CALLED THE *ORESTEIA*

THE story of the House of Atreus was well known. It involved persons and events which were at least as popular and as romantic as any in the Greek legends. Some of its episodes and situations made the strongest appeal to the passions and sympathies of men.

Moreover, this story presented questions of the utmost importance to every thinking person:

(a) What is God?

(b) Why must men suffer?

(c) What is sin?

(d) If suffering is punishment for sin, why do the innocent suffer as well as the guilty?

(e) Can two standards of right conflict? Does God ever command what is wrong in itself?

(f) Are some acts sinful in themselves, irrespective of motive or circumstances?

With some of these questions Aeschylus deals in this trilogy. He does not define his conception of God. He seems to assume that a Supreme God, Zeus, exists, and perhaps also other gods: if so, then the other gods are subordinate and not powerful except with the consent of Zeus. Of course there cannot be more than one omnipotent being. Thus Aeschylus seems to have been tending towards a monotheistic conception of deity.

Why is there evil in the world (our world), and suffering? Aeschylus seems to have felt that for him there was no escape from this question. In the first chorus of the *Agamemnon* he says that the only solution of this problem he has found is based on his belief in the will of Zeus, who has set this law — at least for men — that knowledge comes by suffering. That is not a very satisfying solution, for the dilemma remains, still, for every man who thinks about such things at all; either this Supreme Being cannot prevent suffering, and then he is not supreme, or else he can prevent suffering but does not, and then he is not good. It does not really help much to say: Goodness in man cannot be defined, much less goodness in God or omnipotence. Can an omnipotent God, for example, cause that which actually has happened to have not happened?

Of course finite minds cannot comprehend infinite goodness or infinite power. But man can understand that unless there were evil as well as good there could be no choice between the two, and without choice there could be no moral character. Gradually, with a slowness which to men is incomprehensible, moral beings seem to be evolving in this world. It is inconceivable — at least to us — that moral beings could be evolved except by choice between good and evil. Dimly we may perhaps apprehend that those who in this world have acquired "knowledge," who have learned to choose good instead of evil, may have a good life in another world, while those who in this present world have not learned to choose the good may have an evil life in a world beyond.

Aeschylus does not define sin. He assumes that there is such a thing as sin, that punishment is a consequence of sin, and that mortals are sometimes agents of God in inflicting punishment. Here, in the story of the House of Atreus, appears a succession of sins and punishments involving at least three generations.

Thyestes sinned in violating the wife of his brother Atreus. For this sin Thyestes suffered at the hands of his brother. Perhaps then Atreus was the agent of Zeus in punishing Thyestes; but, if so, he must have exceeded his commission, for the pain he inflicted was far greater than the original injury: he killed two of Thyestes' sons, and served their flesh as food for their father to eat. It seems as if Atreus used his office of punisher to satisfy his own personal cruelty and hatred and desire for revenge. So, in punishing, Atreus sinned more grossly than the sinner whom he punished. The sin of Atreus in turn brought on other punishment, namely, the curse laid upon the whole house.

It is not clear from Aeschylus's trilogy, or from the story as we know it otherwise, that Atreus suffered personally in consequence of his own sin. It is not likely that, in the legends before Aeschylus, Atreus's treatment of his brother was regarded as sin necessitating the punishment of Atreus. Nor did Aeschylus develop this idea. Perhaps that was because the acts of Thyestes and Atreus lay outside the scenes of the trilogy. Perhaps these acts were introduced in the form of narrative into the trilogy only to call attention to the continuity of sins and punishments in this preeminent family, and to give occasion for a discussion of the consequences of sin, one of which Aeschylus held to be a propensity in the sinner to further sin. Yet Aeschylus was not a determinist. He held that one sin tends to induce other sins, but that no man is compelled to sin or to sin again. When a man has committed a sin, part of his punishment consists in a propensity to sin again; but every man can extricate himself, if he will.

In the first drama of this trilogy Aeschylus has more to say about Helen than about Paris, but perhaps only because her part seemed to him more inexcusable or more dramatic. The sin of Paris and Helen led to immense suffering by both Trojans and Greeks; but not simply because he was a Trojan and she was a Greek — or was commonly regarded as a Greek. Their sin involved the Trojans perhaps because they received Paris back into their city, and with him his wife, stolen from Menelaus, and her jewels. To punish the Trojans Agamemnon was sent by Zeus as his agent to execute his judgment. But in acting as the agent of Zeus, Agamemnon sought also his own glory, and thus became himself a sinner. Agamemnon's sin involved many Greeks who stayed at home, as well as those who went on the expedition. It seems to me that, in the first choral ode of the *Agamemnon,* Aeschylus makes it clear that this was his belief. But apparently he found it hard to understand why all the Trojans suffered for the sin of Paris and many of the Greeks suffered for the sin of Agamemnon. The chorus does assert that the Trojans received Helen gladly and refused to give her up, thereby accepting responsibility for the sin of Paris. In those times they could hardly have done otherwise, and in any case such a war might have occurred for no other reason than the desire of one group of people to conquer another. Such wars are common enough. The chorus also implies that many of the Greeks followed Agamemnon gladly and, for the sake of adventure or lust or loot, made themselves willing accessories to Agamemnon's ruthless violence and participants in his sin. But many, both of the Trojans and of the Greeks, had nothing to say about the war at all; they did not choose to fight. If those, who as individuals caused a war by some provocative act or were the aggressors in a war of conquest, were punished individually, that could be understood. But how can anyone understand why those suffer who had no part in causing a war, or who fought only to defend their homes? Whatever he may have thought, Aeschylus does not say that war — even a war of aggression — is wrong. Perhaps he believed that war with all its attendant suffering and horror belongs to the inevitable vicissitudes of life. He does imply, however, that this Trojan war was occasioned by the sins of certain individuals, and that in general, the sin of an individual brings not only punishment to the sinner but also suffering to persons innocent of the sin. It is a fact in human life that suffering falls upon those apparently innocent as well as upon the guilty. Of this fact

Aeschylus, in this trilogy, offers no explanation unless it is in the belief, mentioned above, that knowledge (i.e. moral perception?) is developed in men through suffering.

About the sin of Agamemnon and its punishment, however, Aeschylus makes his opinion clear. Agamemnon was commissioned to execute the judgment of Zeus upon Paris and the Trojans. He used this commission for his own glory and personal advantage. When adverse winds delayed the sailing of his fleet, he did not inquire what was the will of Zeus, or what was the judgment which he, Agamemnon, was sent to execute. He asked only how he could assuage the winds, so that the fleet might sail and that he might conquer Troy. The prophet told him that if he sacrificed his daughter the fleet would sail and he would conquer. Agamemnon had no command from Zeus to sacrifice Iphigenia. Ruthlessly and cruelly, in order to gratify his own ambition and desire he sacrificed his daughter, neglected his kingdom and his home, destroyed a great city, lost many of his own people, killed or enslaved every Trojan. Therefore he was punished.

During Agamemnon's long absence his wife, Clytemnestra, conspired against him with his cousin Aegisthus, son of that Thyestes who had been so cruelly treated by Agamemnon's father Atreus. It may be that Aegisthus's claim to the throne was really better than Agamemnon's, for perhaps Aegisthus's father was the older son; that may have been in the legend, but it is not stated in the play, and would not, in either case, have affected the issues with which Aeschylus is dealing here. On Agamemnon's return, he with his slave Cassandra, the youngest and fairest of the daughters of the king of Troy, was treacherously killed. According to the story as told by Aeschylus, Clytemnestra killed her husband by her own hand, and Aegisthus with Clytemnestra ruled in Agamemnon's place.

It may be that in killing Agamemnon, Clytemnestra also was acting as an agent of Zeus to punish a sinner. Aeschylus does not say this himself, but in the drama Clytemnestra asserts it explicitly. But if this were true, then Clytemnestra in her turn used her divine commission to attain her own personal ends. She sought for herself revenge on Agamemnon for his neglect of her and for his sacrifice of her daughter. Also she wished to wed Aegisthus and still be queen. Whether in those times to kill anyone for revenge could be regarded as a sin or not, no one even then could doubt that it was sinful for a woman to kill her husband in order to marry his cousin. Therefore, even though she was commissioned by Zeus to punish a sinner, in punishing she sinned herself, and therefore she also was punished.

The punishment of Clytemnestra occupies the second drama of the trilogy. In this drama Orestes, son of Agamemnon and Clytemnestra, was commissioned by the Supreme Being, explicitly and unmistakably, to kill Aegisthus and Clytemnestra in punishment for their sin. This was a most difficult and dangerous, apparently an impossible, task for a young man without an army and with no assistance except that of his sister and of his friend Pylades. But he accomplished it: he killed both of the sinners with his own hand.

In so acting as the agent of Zeus to execute his judgments, did Orestes also exceed his commission? Did he, in punishing, commit sin and incur punishment himself, as the others of his family had? Certainly it could not be counted as a sin for him that he killed Aegisthus who had conspired to kill Orestes' father and had seized the kingdom to which Orestes laid claim. Even though Aegisthus was a kinsman, no one could say justly that in such circumstances Orestes sinned in killing his father's cousin, and no one in this trilogy did say that. It is true that from this killing Orestes had personal profit — he recovered thereby the kingdom of which he had been defrauded. But there is no suggestion anywhere that he acted from this motive: he killed Aegisthus in obedience to a direct command, and there is no implication that otherwise he would have undertaken a venture so hopeless and reckless.

However, Orestes killed his own mother, Clytemnestra. He had no personal advantage from that and sought none. Since Aegisthus was now dead the kingdom belonged to Orestes; no one would have disputed this. He had nothing at all to gain for himself by killing Clytemnestra; he killed her reluctantly, against his own impulse and desire, in obedience to the plain command. But to kill one's own mother was sin, according to primitive ideas, irrespective of the cause or the motive of the act.

The justification of Orestes occupies the third drama ot this trilogy. In interpreting the *Eumenides,* I agree entirely with Verrall in his Introduction to this play.

The story that a son was compelled to kill his mother (originally, I suppose, by the obligation of blood-vengeance) originated in a primitive age and involved the apparent paradox that sometimes it is right for a man to do wrong. To Aeschylus this seemed absurd and repugnant. If Orestes was compelled to kill his mother this could have been only by a command, ultimately from the Supreme Being himself. But if this Supreme Being commanded Orestes to kill his mother, then it could not have been wrong for Orestes to obey. How it was not wrong for Orestes to kill his mother, or how, on the other hand, it was not wrong for Orestes to disobey the command of the Supreme Being, no man can understand. Perhaps Zeus himself or Athena could understand, but men could not.

That is why the court scene is introduced in the *Eumenides*.
The arguments made on each side are not only utterly unconvincing — they are absurd. One might think that Aeschylus
is being sarcastic and wished to make the judicial procedure
at Athens appear ridiculous. But there were no valid arguments which could be made. The facts were admitted by all.
The issue rested squarely on a conflict of authority, which
could not be settled by argument. The case was not judiciable
before any human court, or before the human mind for that
matter. To show that this is so was the sole purpose of this
scene. Still less should anyone suggest that Aeschylus wished
to flatter or please the Athenians by showing a divine origin
for their Court of the Areopagus. The court makes a very
sorry appearance in this scene; it listens to ridiculous arguments and reaches no decision at all. When, by the vote of
Athena, Orestes is formally acquitted and withdraws, the
real question at issue remains as undecided as before. Such
a scene could not have seemed flattering to the Athenians.

Perhaps, however, the legends of the House of Atreus were
not true. That would have been one way out of the dilemma.
Some of the Greek philosophers, such as Heracleitus, chose
this way out of other difficulties which the legends involved.
But not Aeschylus. He did not deny any part of the legends in
which most people of his time believed.

Or perhaps the idea that certain acts are sinful in themselves, irrespective of motive or circumstances, is primitive
and defective. Once this idea was common enough, if not universal. It appears, for example, in the story of Uzzah, told in
2 Samuel vi. 6-7 (*cf.* 1 Sam. vi). It is incorporated in the
legends of the Erinyes, the ministers of an inexorable legality.
To Aeschylus this idea seemed no longer tenable in an age
when motive appeared to be of the very essence of sin.
Accordingly, he believed that the old conception of the
Erinyes must somehow be changed or abandoned. Only, it

did not seem wise to him to preach too openly that the old anthropomorphic conceptions of the gods and the inherited standards of morality should be abandoned.

Throughout the *Oresteia,* as in the *Prometheus Bound,* there are frequent references to a contrast and a conflict between older and newer gods. These newer gods are not the "new and transient" gods of the *Promethus:* they are still more new. The old gods are those who were conceived in a primitive age, the new gods those conceived in a more enlightened age. The trilogy closes with a reconciliation of the old order with the new. This reconciliation is effected by Athena, acting as the representative of the new gods, or by a new Zeus, appealing directly to the representatives of the old order.

Aeschylus accepted the legends of the House of Atreus, and while he added many details of his own imagining, he altered nothing that was traditional in his time. Perhaps he chose these legends as raw material for his *Oresteia* chiefly because of the dramatic situations they offered and because of their emotional appeal. But he seems to have thought that these legends presented extreme but on the whole possible, perhaps even typical, experiences of men. Here was a succession of sins against the prevailing standards of morality, involving cases where one member of a famous family killed some other member of that same family. Thus there came to be a sort of blood-feud perpetuating itself for at least several generations within this family. A blood-feud within a family must have seemed to the ancient Greeks peculiarly horrible. The succession of these killings came to an end with the killing of Clytemnestra by Orestes. At least there was nothing in the legends about Orestes being killed by anyone. Perhaps that was only because these legends ended with the return of Orestes. But Aeschylus sought a reason for this ending. He tried to make sense out of these legends, to find in them an explanation of the suffering in the world, to reach a better understanding of the nature and purposes of God. And this is his conclusion: Man sins because of selfishness, greed or lust. God punishes sin, and in punishing often employs mortals as his agents. These agents, in executing their commissions, often seek their own ends, commit sin themselves, incur punishment in turn. Thus it was in the House of Atreus, until Orestes executed his commission and obeyed the command of God without seeking his own ends and without thereby committing new sin. That ended the chain of sins and punishments in that family.

But there remained far more to explain. Why should God punish sin at all? Why should sinners involve in the punishment for their sin other persons who seem innocent of that sin? Why is there so much suffering in all the world? Aeschylus believed in God, but in a God far removed from the anthropomorphic conceptions of deity current in his time. He believed that God wills that men through suffering learn wisdom, that is, learn to master their selfish desires and submit themselves to Him. That, I think, is as far as Aeschylus went in his thinking about these things, but that is far indeed.

We may go farther still. There is in the natural world an inestimable amount of suffering. Animals suffer, as much as they have capacity for suffering. They are also selfish, greedy and lustful, as far as they have the capacity. That they are benefited in any way or improved by their suffering is not clear to us. But this much is clear: in this world in which pain as well as pleasure is common, sorrow as well as joy, evil as well as good, man has been evolved, superior to the other animals in intelligence and in other qualities. As these qualities in man develop, so his capacity for suffering and for evil increases, but also his capacity for joy and for goodness. And this also seems to me quite clear: it is through the noble endurance of suffering, without bitterness or rancor, and by the struggle against what is evil and for what is good, that the spiritual element in man has been, and is being, developed. We may never understand why there is for us no other way, for human experience shows no other way, and doubtless human experience must always be the ultimate basis of all human reasoning. At least as far as we can know then, there is no other way. Who has ever attained what we call moral character, or has gained some conception of that which is not material but spiritual without the endurance of suffering and sorrow which the sufferer himself is unable to remove, and without the struggle against evil and for the good? Moreover, suffering affects more than those who suffer, for any genuine suffering, but especially suffering bravely endured, speaks to the hearts of all men excepting those completely brutalized, calls men to be more courageous, more understanding, more considerate of others.

But if there is no other way, this at least is a way. Those who endure and struggle for the right develop spiritually and begin to have some knowledge, some comprehension of God.

VII

THE *ANTIGONE* OF SOPHOCLES

THE legends which concerned the city of Thebes in Boeotia included the story of Oedipus, one of its ancient mythical kings, and of his four children, his two daughters, Antigone and Ismene, and his sons, Eteocles and Polyneices. Oedipus, because he had killed his father and married his own mother while unaware of his relationship to them, brought pollution and pestilence upon the city. When the facts were known, Oedipus put out his own eyes and became an exile, accompanied only by his daughter Antigone, leaving his kingdom to his two sons under the guardianship of Creon, their mother's brother. Because these sons showed no affection for him Oedipus laid them under a curse. Consequently, when they became of age and one of them, or both jointly, inherited the kingdom, the brothers quarrelled. Polyneices, apparently the younger brother, left the city, raised an army under six chieftains besides himself, and attacked Eteocles. This expedition was known as the War of the Seven against Thebes In the battle the brothers met and killed each other. Creon then became the king and issued a proclamation that the body of Eteocles should be buried with highest honors, but that the body of Polyneices should be left unburied outside the city walls: any attempt to bury the traitor's body was forbidden under penalty of death. Antigone, however, who had returned to Thebes after her father's death, defied Creon's edict, performed over the body of her brother the rites necessary to secure for him passage to the place of departed spirits, and was condemned to death by Creon. In Sophocles' play, Haemon, Creon's only son, is in love with Antigone, and when he is unable to save her, takes his own life, causing his mother Eurydice to kill herself in grief; but it is not certain whether these deaths were in any legend before Sophocles or not.

These legends furnished the situation on which the *Antigone* of Sophocles was based: a decree by a legitimate sovereign conflicts with custom and moral obligation; a subject of the sovereign disobeys this decree; the sovereign then finds himself involved in a dilemma from which he cannot escape, and is ultimately ruined.

The play opens with the appearance of two young women, who come out of the stage-building. Their conversation immediately shows that they are Antigone and Ismene, and that the stage-building represents the palace of the kings of Thebes. Antigone is on her way to perform the rites of burial over the body of Polyneices, in defiance of Creon's edict; she invites her sister to go with her and to share in this undertaking. The limitations of the Greek theater of course made it necessary that this conversation should take place in the orchestra, although to a modern reader this seems most unnatural. Ismene refuses to join in this disobedience and returns to the palace, while Antigone in anger goes on alone through the passage on the spectators' left which leads to the open country outside the city's walls. Ismene shows herself rather weak and easygoing, but not wholly lacking in affection. Antigone is strong-minded, opinionated, somewhat bitter and fanatical, and not altogether averse to a martyr's rôle.

When both have disappeared, the chorus consisting of Theban elders enters through the passage on the right and sings a long ode: they have been summoned to the palace. Creon then appears, announces that he is now the king, and makes proclamation of his edict. The elders profess acceptance of his authority and obedience to his commands, though without expressing their approval. Just then a soldier enters from the left. He is one of those sent to watch the body of Polyneices and to prevent any attempt to bury it. He is a somewhat comic figure, and his rather boorish humor re-

lieves the tension. He tells that someone has already performed the essential rites of burial over the corpse, and has
escaped undetected. Creon is irascible and appears not quite
sure of himself. He defends his edict and claims to see in
this disobedience to his orders evidence that there are still
traitors in Thebes. He suggests that the guards have been
bribed. He orders the soldier to return to his post at once,
and threatens that if the guards do not immediately find and
arrest the persons who performed the forbidden rites, the
guards themselves will be executed with torture. He then
retires, probably into the palace, the soldier returns to his
place, and the chorus sings one of the most beautiful odes in
the Greek drama, extolling obedience to constituted authority.

Presently the soldier reappears, bringing with him Antigone, a prisoner. Creon comes out from the palace, and the
soldier tells him that the guards laid bare the corpse again
and sat down at some little distance to watch. While they
were temporarily blinded by a dust storm Antigone came
and once more sprinkled earth upon the body. But this time
she did not escape, and the same soldier was sent to bring
her to the king. The soldier is dismissed and retires at once.
Creon questions Antigone, who confesses proudly that she
disobeyed the king's order and defends her action. He accuses Ismene of complicity in what he considers a crime: he
sends for her also, and she is led out from the palace by
attendants. Apparently somewhat ashamed of her former
attitude, or else believing that Creon will not dare to execute
both princesses who are the sole survivors of the royal family,
Ismene claims that she participated in Antigone's action and
so should share in the consequences. But Antigone denies
this claim angrily and bitterly. Perhaps, however, though she
appeared to be really angry when Ismene refused to cooperate,
she now only feigns anger against her sister in order to convince Creon that Ismene had no part in the matter and there-

fore cannot be punished with any semblance of justice. Creon
is unwilling to make any concession, and orders the attendants to conduct both the maidens into the palace, he himself
remaining outside, while the chorus sings of the misfortunes
of the house of Oedipus.

Then Haemon, the son of Creon and betrothed to Antigone, arrives from somewhere in the city, and tries to persuade his father to pardon Antigone. At·first he speaks re-
spectfully and tactfully, while Creon argues with him. The
elders weakly agree that there is reason on both sides. But
finally both father and son become very angry. Haemon says
that the Thebans do not approve of the king's intention.
Creon asks if the people should dictate to him. Haemon
replies that a state which belongs to one man is no state at
all. Creon says that Haemon shall never marry Antigone
and that she must die. At last Haemon goes off in a rage.
The chorus asks whether both the girls are to be killed. The
king agrees that one is innocent and decides that she shall
be spared, but that Antigone shall be punished. Since she is of
his own kindred he cannot kill her directly, but will have her
walled up alive in a rock-hewn chamber, remote from the
town, where she will soon die of starvation. The chorus sings
of love and its power over men. Then Antigone is brought
out and, in a most moving dialogue with the chorus, laments
her approaching death, until Creon interrupts and Antigone
is led away by guards.

The chorus sings of the dreadful power of fate — whatever that may be — citing instances known to all from the
familiar legends, in which unjust cruelties were inflicted
on men or women by other mortals. Then the blind and aged
seer Teiresias appears, warns Creon that he is making a
mistake, pleads with him to relent, and finally threatens him,
prophesying the death of Haemon. When the prophet has

left, Creon seems uncertain and somewhat frightened. And now the elders, for the first time, take an independent attitude, express their own opinion; they urge the king to release the maiden, and to bury the body of Polyneices in a proper tomb. This is too much for Creon, for now everyone is against him. He yields and, with his attendants, goes immediately to carry out his new resolution.

The chorus now sings an ode, invoking the god Dionysus to deliver the city from the calamities which have been fore-told by Teiresias. The singing of the ode indicates to the audience that the passage of a certain, not very long, time must be imagined between the last scene and the next. Presently a messenger appears and tells that Haemon is dead. Eurydice, Haemon's mother, comes out, apparently from the palace, and hears the messenger's story. He says that Creon went first to the place where Polyneices' body lay, and with the appropriate ceremonies burned the corpse, buried the ashes and raised above them a barrow. Then all went to the chamber where Antigone was confined. There they found that An-tigone had hanged herself, and that Haemon was clasping her dead body in a frenzy of grief. When Creon approached, Haemon attempted to kill his father but, failing in his at-tempt, killed himself with his sword. Hearing this Eurydice retires into the palace, followed by the messenger. Creon comes back with attendants carrying the body of Haemon. Antigone's body is not brought home, and nothing more is said about her except by the messenger, who later reports that Eurydice blamed Creon for the death of both her son and her son's betrothed. The messenger returns and tells that Eurydice too has killed herself. The stricken Creon enters the palace with the household servants, if any are then present, while the chorus and all others retire towards the city.

[79]

The issue involved in this drama is commonly regarded as one between law and right. Is it ever morally right for a person to break the law of his country or to disobey an edict of his sovereign? Doubtless in some circumstances it is; but always this must be a difficult question for any individual to reason out intellectually. Was it really right for Antigone to disobey Creon's decree? Was her decision determined by a genuine moral obligation, or merely by convention, family pride, personal vanity, desire to play a heroic rôle, or some such consideration? There is talk in the play of affection between Antigone and Polyneices; but I see no evidence of real affection between the two. The assertion of affection seems to me a false note in the play, unless it is regarded merely as an explanation offered by Antigone because she thought it the most easily understood. Elsewhere Antigone talks about the ordinances of the gods as of more binding authority than those of men. This seems to me the chief issue, but if so, it is complicated and obscured by other issues. I do not think that Sophocles considered either the moral or the political implications of the story at all; he makes no attempt to solve any of the problems which the story presents. He chose for the subject of this tragedy a most tragic situation, which led to the pitiful ruin of all the principal characters concerned — a story which would affect most strongly the emotions of his audience. He does not show that either Antigone or Creon was right or wrong. All the other characters in the play sympathize with the former against the latter, and finally Teiresias, who seems to represent the judgment of the gods, sternly condemns the attitude of Creon. But this condemnation seems to relate partly to a certain impiety in Creon's treatment of Polyneices' corpse but chiefly to the severity of Antigone's punishment. Haemon denies the right of a sovereign to make arbitrary decisions contrary to the will of his people, and certainly this was the popular

opinion at Athens in the time of Sophocles. But it can hardly
have been held by many in the time of the ancient Greek
kings. Creon expresses the opposite opinion, and his attitude
is much the same as that exhibited in the correspondence
between Queen Victoria and her daughter, the Empress
Frederick. Of course, in most modern audiences sympathy
would remain with Antigone throughout. She makes a decision which she believes to be right for her, and dies for it.
Creon makes a decision and, though later he reverses that
decision, he is left desolate. I have the impression that if
Sophocles himself had been placed in such circumstances he
would have agreed with Ismene. Perhaps he would have said:
"In general, it is better not to issue orders which conflict
with what people believe to be right, or with custom or tradition or religion." But if he had been there himself I think
he would have obeyed the edict without hesitation. It is the
tragic situations themselves with which Sophocles is concerned, not the solution of any problems involved. The same
can be said of his *Oedipus Tyrannus* and his *Philoctetes*.
Herein Sophocles differs greatly from Aeschylus.

Antigone's problem is presented also to Ismene, and thus
both sides of this question are developed. Creon's problem,
whether to rescind his decree or not, is discussed by Haemon
with his father, and thus both sides of that question are
represented.

Antigone and Creon have certain salient faults in common.
Both are opinionated, obstinate, and influenced by personal
vanity. Antigone persists perhaps because she is cantankerous
by nature or hardened by her experiences in the past. Certainly she is a bit fanatical. Creon persists in his course perhaps because he is really weak, and, like many who are not
quite sure of themselves, afraid to change his mind. But
for each of them there is genuinely a principle at stake, in
the one case that moral obligation exceeds legal obligation,

in the other case that authority must be enforced for the good of society as a whole. Antigone may well have believed that she was under a moral obligation to perform for her dead brother the ritual of burial, at least in its essential elements, since otherwise his spirit would wander eternally outside that realm in which the buried dead were believed to have some sort of an existence. Creon may well have believed that if he failed to enforce his decree, or wavered in any way, disorder and more bloodshed would ensue. From the conflict of these principles Sophocles suggests no way of escape.

An interesting parallel to the story of Antigone is furnished by the account of Maria Montalti in *My Reminiscences,* by Raphael Pumpelly, quoted by Professor J. T. Allen in *Classical Journal,* Vol. XXXIII (1938), No. 4.

As is usual in the plays of Sophocles, the character of each person in the *Antigone* is well and carefully drawn as far as it affects or is affected by the situation in which that person participates, but not otherwise. Thus there is no attempt here to portray these persons as it were "in the round." Perhaps Teiresias here serves, not as a person or character at all, but only as the visible representative of an other-worldly standard.

Creon is the central figure. He alone is present practically throughout the entire play, and at the end he alone remains of all the principal persons except Ismene, who does not seem to have been present in the last scene. Each person in the cast serves to exhibit in some way the consequences of Creon's decision, made before the play begins.

There is no similarity between the Creon of the *Antigone* and the Creon of the *Oedipus Tyrannus.* The opinion of some, that in the later play Sophocles wished to show in an earlier stage of development the kind of person who might have become the Creon of the *Antigone* when he in turn became the monarch, seems to me without foundation. There are, however, some striking similarities, though no evident identity, between the character of Creon in the *Antigone* and of Oedipus in the *Oedipus Tyrannus*. If behind these two characters there was some real person — Pericles, perhaps — we have no means of knowing that this is so, or who that person was. Not infrequently Sophocles used in a later play characters, ideas, and even expressions of an earlier play. So there is a good deal of similarity between the Teiresias in the *Antigone* and the Teiresias in the *Oedipus Tyrannus*. So also in the *Electra* of Sophocles, which was later than the *Antigone,* there is a pair of sisters who are contrasted; only, Ismene in the *Antigone* and Chrysothemis in the *Electra* are rather more alike than Antigone and Electra themselves.

In considering the construction of this play certain questions arise, which are important enough for any complete criticism, but are such that only subjective and uncertain answers to them can be given.

1. Why did Antigone perform the ritual of burial for Polyneices twice? For the natural development of the plot she might have been caught the first time. Was it only to give occasion for that somewhat humorous scene between Creon and the soldier, and to exhibit Creon's character in one more episode? Was it to show that Antigone was really a fanatic, anxious to be caught and to be made a martyr? Or was it because she was afraid that the wind had somehow nullified the rite which she had performed, perhaps without sufficient thoroughness, and therefore did she risk her life a second time to make sure? Psychologically, I think this explanation sound enough; but I find no hint in the play itself that Sophocles considered this the real motive for Antigone's second visit. Perhaps Sophocles counted on more subtilty and

imagination in his audience than most modern readers bring to the study of these plays.

2. Why did Creon bury the body of Polyneices, when all that was ritually essential had already been done? Was he uncertain whether this had been done sufficiently? Of course, when Creon buried the body he did it thoroughly, in a grave. That had its importance. But there seems to have been something more about this. Perhaps Sophocles wished to show that Creon's repentance was sincere, and that he now acknowledged publicly that he ought to have buried the body originally. After all, the burying or not burying of that body had made all the trouble. It is a pity that his change of mind was made too late.

3. Why did Creon bury Polyneices before he went to release Antigone? Perhaps if he had not done so he would have arrived at the tomb in time to save the girl, and so the prophecy of Teiresias would have proved untrue. But perhaps the prophecy would not have been unfulfilled anyway. Antigone might have taken her life immediately, as soon as she was left alone, while Creon was still talking with Teiresias, and Haemon might have killed himself whenever Creon appeared after Antigone's death. Was it rather, as some critics have said, Jebb for example, merely so that the effective and affecting narrative of the messenger might not end in an anticlimax, the burying of a miserable corpse following after the tragic deaths of the royal lovers? But would this have been an anticlimax? If Creon, even after the death of Antigone and Haemon, had still gone on, stoically and doggedly, to bury the body of Polyneices, would that not have been very impressive indeed? I think that the reason why he went first to bury the dead was that in the play as Sophocles wrote it the burying of the body was the important thing.

4. Why is the love of Antigone and Haemon kept so consistently in the background? An answer to this question would involve an understanding of the most obvious but to us the most enigmatic feature of the ancient Greek tragedies, and in fact of all the classical Greek literature. The matter has often been studied and commented upon, especially in recent times, but it has never been clear to me.

5. Why is Haemon's body brought to the palace, but not the body of Antigone?

6. Why does Eurydice appear in this play at all? She is not necessary to the plot, and doubtless was not mentioned in the original legend, any more than Aegeus belonged in the story of how Medea killed her children.

The same answer applies to both of these last two questions. Haemon's body is brought back to the palace alone and Eurydice appears and then takes her own life in order to present more vividly to the audience the catastrophe which befell Creon.

That is another indication that this play is primarily about Creon and his calamity. It must be remembered that the titles of these plays which have come down to us do not in all cases indicate the chief character. The titles seem to me to have been chosen primarily to indicate what legend was the basis of the play. For example, if the play by Euripides, which is about Admetus but is called the *Alcestis,* had been called *Admetus,* any Greek reading this title would have expected a dramatization of the story of the king in whose household the god Apollo had been a servant for a year. The title *Alcestis* suggested a drama about the king whose wife died for him. Perhaps these titles were posted up somewhere before the performance of the plays, and so were, to some extent, substitutes for our modern programs. The same thing applies also to the *Antigone,* which is primarily a drama about Creon and his dilemma.

VIII

THE *OEDIPUS TYRANNUS* OF SOPHOCLES

A. THE OEDIPUS-LEGEND

THE date of the *Antigone* is not definitely known. It is generally believed that it was produced about 442 B.C., and there are some good but not entirely convincing reasons for that date. The date of the *Oedipus Tyrannus,* i.e. *Oedipus the King,* may be 425 B.C., though this also is uncertain. The allusions in the play to the plague at Thebes caused by the pollution brought by Oedipus, and the picture given of conditions in the plague-stricken city are so detailed and so vivid, that it seems to me clear that the play must have been written after the real plague from which Athens suffered in 430 B.C. and in the following year. If that is so, then the *Oedipus Tyrannus* was later than the *Antigone,* probably by fifteen years or more. Perhaps the play originally was called simply the *Oedipus.* Afterwards (after Sophocles' death), *Tyrannus* was added to the title in order to distinguish this play from the *Oedipus Coloneus,* or *Oedipus on Colonus,* which is said to have been produced after Sophocles' death, in 401 B.C.

It is not possible to determine how far Sophocles in constructing his plot was dependent upon the legends already current. When he wrote this play the common version of the legend among the Athenians seems to have been this. Oedipus, the son of Laïus and Iocasta, the king and queen of Thebes, was for some reason brought up from infancy by Polybus and Merope, the king and queen of Corinth. When Oedipus became of age, i.e. probably eighteen, someone insinuated that he was not the son of Polybus. Oedipus asked Polybus and Merope whose son he really was, but they would not give him a direct answer. He then applied to the oracle at Delphi; the oracle did not say who his parents were, but foretold that he would kill his father and marry his mother. Believing that Polybus and Merope were his parents, and naturally wishing to avoid the fulfillment of the prophecy if this were in any way possible, Oedipus refused to return to Corinth and took the road which led in the opposite direction. This was the road to Thebes. On the way he met his father who in a carriage with four attendants was going to Delphi to consult the oracle about the sphinx, a monster which appeared every day in Thebes, propounded a riddle and, when the riddle was not solved, carried off a son of one of the noblest families. Of course neither father nor son recognized the other. An altercation on the road occurred and Oedipus killed Laïus and three of his attendants; the fourth escaped. When Oedipus reached Thebes, the news of the king's death had already arrived, and the Thebans had issued a proclamation that whoever offered himself as their champion, solved the riddle propounded to him, and so rid the city of the sphinx, should succeed to the kingdom and should marry the widowed queen. She might have been not more than thirty-five years old at that time. Oedipus, now a soldier of fortune, believing that he had nothing to lose but his life and eager for a chance to win a kingdom, offered himself as the champion. He met the sphinx and guessed her riddle: What is it that is two-footed, and four-footed, and three-footed, and is feeblest the more feet it goes upon? The sphinx disappeared, and Oedipus became king of Thebes and married the queen, who was really his mother, although of course she was quite unknown to him. When four children had been born, the city was visited by a devastating pestilence. When all the facts were made known, Iocasta committed suicide, Oedipus blinded himself, or was blinded, and went into exile accompanied by his daughter Antigone.

As the story grew, an explanation was furnished for the incident that Oedipus did not grow up at home; an oracle declared to Laïus that he would be killed by his son, and therefore, when a son was born to him, the son was immediately exposed on a mountain to die, but was rescued by some shepherds, taken to Corinth, and there adopted by the king who was childless. An explanation for this oracle was also provided by the supposition that Laïus had sinned against the gods by carrying off Chrysippus, a son of Pelops, to gratify his lust. Therefore, the gods foretold to Laïus that there would be no natural relationships in his family, and that if he had a son this son would cause his death. Of course, the introduction of homosexuality as the primary cause of all the troubles of this family is comparatively late, and perhaps some of the other details, including the adoption of Oedipus by the king of Corinth, are late too.

The legend of Oedipus was very old, and very familiar to all the Greeks of the fifth century B.C. The name occurs in the *Iliad* (XXIII, 679 *f.*). There is a brief summary of the story, without mention of the sphinx, in the *Odyssey* (XI, 271-280). It was contained in the ancient epics called the *Cypria,* the *Thebaïs* and the *Oedipodeia.* Poets, such as Pindar, spoke of it, and historians such as Hellanicus and Pherecydes included it in their narratives. Aeschylus based a trilogy upon it. The whole story, with certain variations and most of the accretions, including the quarrel and death of Oedipus's sons and the disobedience and punishment of Antigone, is told in Apollodorus's *Bibliotheca* (III, 5-7); but in this account the various versions of the legends are combined with the inventions of the poets and dramatists, including Sophocles and Euripides. There are also many illustrations of the Oedipus story in ancient Greek art.

Essentially, the Oedipus legend was that a man killed his father, delivered a city from a monster called a sphinx, and married his mother. These three constituent elements in the complicated legend known in the fifth century may once have existed separately and, since very early legends are commonly very simple, it is probable that one of them is the

original Oedipus legend and that the others were attached to
it later. When we inquire which of them was the original
story of Oedipus, it becomes evident that the first is not the
original one.

That a father and son, not recognizing each other, engage in mortal combat is a story found among practically
all Indo-European peoples. Perhaps the best example is
the German story of Hildebrand and his son Hadubrand.
An exhaustive discussion of this legend may be found in
an article by Bruno Busse, entitled "Sagengeschichtliches
zum Hildebrandsliede," in the periodical called *Beiträge zur
Geschichte der deutschen Sprache und Literatur*, Vol. XXVI
(1901), pp. 1-92. The same story is told of Rustem and his
son Zohrab among the Persians, although in this case, as in
some others, it is the son who is killed. This is the subject of
the well known poem of Matthew Arnold. Dr. Busse cites
among many other examples the Russian legend of Igla von
Murom, who kills his son Sbuta, and the English legend of
Eglamour of Artoys who meets his son Deglabell (his mother
was Crystabell) in a tourney. Among the Greeks the legend
is found in the story of Odysseus's death at the hands of
Telegonus, his son by Circe; in the story of the founding of
Tenedos, in which Tennes kills his father Cycnus; in the
story of Althaemenes who kills his father Catreus (Apollod.
III,2,2,3); in the story of Perseus and his grandfather Acri-
sius, and of Meleager and his grandfather Thestius.

It is evident then, that this legend belongs to Indo-European
folk-lore and existed independently of the name Oedipus.
Nor does there appear to be any connection between the name
and the story. The name is Greek and the legend existed before there was a Greek folk. Nor is the name derived in any
way from or explained in any way by the story. Nor is Oedipus by any means the only person associated with this story

even among the Greeks. We must conclude, therefore, that this legend was attached to Oedipus after he had become known for some other reason.

This conclusion is confirmed by the fact that in the oldest version of the Oedipus legend as we know it, in the Nekuia (*Odyssey,* XI, 271 *ff.*), the killing of the father is mentioned in one half-line only, and that as if an afterthought (perhaps it is actually a late addition) without any vital connection with the rest. Even in Sophocles the killing of the father proves in the end not the most tragic element in the situation.

The second element in the developed story of Oedipus has to do with the sphinx and her riddle. The oldest sphinxes we know are Egyptian. The most notable of all is the colossal sphinx at Gizeh, carved out of living rock, sixty-six feet from the pavement on which it couches to the top of its head, and with a temple between its paws. It has the figure of a lion and a human head. The head is that of a man, bearded, wearing the royal turban decorated with the royal serpent. Such figures symbolized power and majesty. Gods were represented in this form, and kings; the sphinx at Gizeh is generally thought to represent some king of the Fourth Dynasty, 2900-2750 B.C., perhaps Chephren or Mycerinus. Later some sphinxes had wings, but none of these is considered to be earlier than about 1600 B.C. The wings may be due to Assyrian influence, and the winged sphinxes may be regarded as a cross between the majestic and royal lion-man of Egypt and the winged demon of Assyria. There is some evidence indicating that this crossbreeding took place in Phoenicia, where Egyptian and Assyrian art met together. Anyway, winged sphinxes multiplied rapidly in all the ancient world, in Egypt, Assyria, Phoenicia, Asia Minor, the Aegean islands, Greece and Etruria. One of the best examples of a winged sphinx of the earliest type, in marble, was found at Spata in Attica. Others were found at Mycenae, dating from about 1500 B.C., and at least one, in terra cotta, at Thebes. But this archaic sphinx found at Thebes is altogether Egyptian in its type, and has no necessary bearing on the connection between sphinxes and the Theban legends. These archaic sphinxes seem to have symbolized irresistible, perhaps demoniacal, power.

But in Greece another strain was bred into the sphinxes. The Greeks had their own irresistible demons. These were winged beings, commonly female, though sometimes apparently sexless, who carried off mortals. Sometimes one is pictured as a beautiful woman, carrying in her arms the figure of a man. Sometimes they are represented in more revolting shape, as for example the harpies, with the heads and breasts of women but the bodies and talons of birds. The sirens which Ulysses and his companions saw seem to have had the same significance. All of these figures, even the harpies, seem to have been symbols of death. So in Homer (*Odyssey* I, 241) it is said: "But now the harpies have carried him off ingloriously." The concept of these half-human beings which symbolized death seems to have been combined with that of the winged beast which symbolized demoniacal power, so that, at least after the Mycenaean period, the sphinx is generally represented as a winged lion, with the head and breast of a woman. Such sphinxes were common in Attica in the sixth century B.C. as grave monuments, sometimes seated on freestanding columns. They formed part of the decoration of the gold-and-ivory statue of Zeus at Olympia. They are also found on Corinthian vases, painted as carrying off mortals. See R. C. Jebb, *Oedipus Tyrannus,* pp. 226 *ff*.

A possible connection between such a sphinx and Thebes has been suggested by Jebb. There was a mountain in Boeotia called the *phikion oros*, which seems to mean *Shudder Mountain*. Zeus did not mind stopping there once on his way

from Olympia to Thebes, nor did the terrors of this mountain
disturb his thoughts (Hesiod: *Aspis,* 32 *ff.*). But for men it
was a bad place to be about in. Hesiod, early in the seventh
century, knew about the "phix," a horrible monster which
lived on Shudder Mountain. No one seems ever to have seen
the phix or to have known just what it looked like; but then
no one had ever seen a real sphinx either. The names sounded
very much alike, and this may have suggested that these
creatures were a good deal alike too. Perhaps, then, the
monster of the phikion oros began to appear — in works of
art of course — as an ordinary sphinx, with a lion's body,
paws and tail, a woman's head, breast and tongue, and
angel's wings. But, if so, it is not likely to have occurred
much before the end of the seventh century, because Hesiod
does not seem to have known how the phix appeared.

Of course it is possible that the original Oedipus legend
told that he slew the monster of the phikion oros. But Oedipus does not seem like an ordinary slayer of monsters, and
so like Hercules or Perseus or St. George. No other stories
were ever told about his killing any other monsters. Moreover,
in the story of Oedipus and the sphinx, what he actually did
to the beast seems to have been of minor importance. He
guessed her riddle and she then disappeared. Some said that
he killed her or that she killed herself; but others said that she
went back to the mountain, or that the god who had sent her
called her off again, so to speak. So there was no fixed tradition that Oedipus killed any monster. The story of how he
got rid of the sphinx is inseparable from the story of the
riddle. There is no evidence at all in literature or in art that
any such story was thought of before the sixth century B.C.
That was the age of proverbs and riddles, the age of the
Seven Wise Men — the names of about fourteen of whom
are known — the age which produced a great crop of pithy
and witty sayings, many of which became vastly popular for

a time and had a wide circulation. It may be concluded, therefore, that the story of the riddle of the sphinx was invented
in the sixth century. Of course that is a long while ago now.
But the story of how Oedipus married his mother was very
old before the sixth century began. Consequently, it looks as
if the very common story of a man who killed his father,
and the comparatively late story of a man who guessed a
riddle and thereby saved a city, were attached to the original
Oedipus legend to explain how Oedipus came to win his
mother's hand in marriage.

There remains, therefore, as the original Oedipus legend,
the story of the man who married his own mother. Such a
story of incest is not unique in the Greek mythology; it was
told of some other heroes also, and of some of the highest
gods as well. Were not the many incestuous loves of Zeus
notorious? Did not Zeus wed his sister, Hera, and another
sister, Demeter, too? He even wed Persephone, his own
daughter by Demeter, and begot of her a son. And what an
innumerable host of nymphs and mortal maidens Zeus took
unto himself, to some of whom, at least, he was already
bound by other ties! Zeus should have known better, and
should not have furnished such food for the baser imaginations of his people, such scandalous material for the tribes
of poets, artists, and the like.

The Greeks of the historical age were shocked by such
stories, as well as we; many regarded them as relics of a
barbarous age, or as lying inventions of lewd-minded poets,
and some — these were philosophers, of course — were for
throwing overboard as immoral the whole lot of these
anthropomorphic stories of the gods, despite the fact that
some of them were in Homer. But there were some few,
and among them, I think, Sophocles, who understood that
many of these objectionable stories were originally naïve
allegories of certain natural phenomena, which were told first

among a primitive and childlike people who were not in the least shocked by them, but which were often, perhaps from the very beginning, interpreted too literally. There is really a very obvious symbolism in many of these legends. Zeus was originally the personified Sky, as his name seems to imply, and as does certainly such an expression as *Zeus rains.* From him descended, in dew and rain, the fructifying moisture on his sister the Earth, or upon Mother Nature, or upon this glade or that meadow, and so begot nature's offspring. Surely that was the original meaning of the legend of Zeus's wedlock with Demeter, and of the birth of Persephone. For Demeter is Mother Nature herself, or the personification of plant life as a whole, whose child, begotten of the fructifying moisture, is the vegetation of each year, which is born anew each springtime from the old body of plant life, only to be carried off each autumn by the Lord of the World of the Dead. Similarly there are stories in the Greek mythology which represent allegorically the life of the plants or trees.

The original Oedipus legend seems to have been such a nature allegory. If so, it belonged to a primitive age, and to a highly imaginative people who, in their fancy, assigned human characteristics to everything which had life. The later Greeks, however, were shocked by it. To most of Sophocles' audience Oedipus was little more than a man who had, through no fault of his own, a very horrible experience which might happen to anyone, but from which all would hope to be delivered. His calamities were especially tragic because he had always lived a brave and noble life, had been a wise and strong ruler, and had done great service to mankind. Sophocles represents him as an affectionate husband and father, and a king who was really loved, trusted and venerated by his people. In this drama, at least, he appears as one of those figures on whom were laid the burdens and sorrows of the human race, even to the extent of supreme suffering of mind and body, and a shameful end, that others might be spared. The ending of Seneca's *Oedipus,* the whole of which was taken largely from Sophocles, makes it very clear that, for Seneca at least, Oedipus expiated the sins of his people and took upon himself their punishment, so that by his stripes they were healed. Such figures seem, in some degree, to foreshadow the conception of Christ sanctioned by the Christian Church.

Oedipus appeared to Sophocles' audience as little more than a mortal man. Yet there was something mysterious, perhaps supernatural, about him too. His end in particular was not a natural death. No one knew what ultimately became of Oedipus, though there was at least one grave which some believed to have been his. But always it was felt that there was some strange connection between this hero and the dark powers of the Lower World. Perhaps this feeling was only an unconscious survival of the primitive conception of his person. Perhaps it was because people knew that in certain places Oedipus was still worshiped as a god.

The original Oedipus legend belongs among the legends of the Chthonic deities, or Earth-Gods. In its earliest form I think it was this: Oedipus in infancy was cast out, apparently to die. Saved by the will of the gods, even though in the story the rescue of the child was effected through human agency, after long absence and struggling he returned to his own again and saved his people. But when he had reached the fullness of his power, he inseminated the mother who bore him, and thereupon he disappeared in some mysterious way. Sophocles, in the *Oedipus Coloneus,* says that in the end some god called him and he passed from the sight of men. In this respect he was like Enoch, who "walked with God: and he was not; for God took him" (Genesis v. 24). But Oedipus had already entered into darkness, for his eyes had been put out: already he had returned to suffering and abandonment apart from the homes of men. Here are exactly those strange contrasts, those alternations of light and darkness, of joy and sorrow, of strength and weakness, which are characteristic of the legends of Chthonic deities. Moreover, this particular legend, as a whole, is perfectly comprehensible as an allegory of a natural phenomenon, the life of a seed-bearing, deciduous plant, such as a stalk of wheat. At birth the seed is cast out upon the earth, apparently to die. But by some mysterious power it is not only preserved, but transformed into a plant like its father. As such it takes its father's place, for the benefit of mankind. When, in its turn, it reaches maturity, it lets its seed fall upon the earth its mother, and thereupon it disappears.

This interpretation explains what is most peculiar in the legends of Oedipus, and what seems otherwise inexplicable, namely his swollen feet, and his name *Oedipus,* i.e. *Swell-Foot.* For the foot of a plant is the root, which swells when the plant begins to grow. In Sophocles' version of the story Laïus, the father, when he had the child exposed on the mountain to die, had a pin thrust through its ankles, doubtless so that no one would be willing to rescue a child who was likely to be a cripple. But the child was rescued, and its wounded ankles were healed by Merope, its foster mother. Later in this story the damage done to the child's ankles was the clue by which its true mother, Iocasta, found that her husband, Oedipus, was the same person as the baby which she herself had borne and which Laïus had had exposed. But these details are undoubtedly secondary, and were invented to account for the deformed ankles of the man. The interpretation given above accounts also for the triumphs of Oedipus over his vicissitudes, for the benefits which he brought to his

people, for his incestuous marriage, his catastrophe, his blind-
ing, his suffering and disappearance, and for the fact that
he did not die a human death. These things are all parts
of the same allegory, and easily understandable if it is recognized that Oedipus was a personification of plant life, and
so, to some extent, a counterpart of Dionysus himself.

IX

THE *OEDIPUS TYRANNUS* OF SOPHOCLES

B. THE PLAY ITSELF

THE *Oedipus Tyrannus* begins with the entrance into the orchestra, through the passage on the spectators' right, of a procession formed of priests and of boys dressed as young nobles. An aged priest is their leader and later on speaks for them. But this is not the chorus of the play. Before the stage-building is an altar, such as might be in front of any temple or any palace. If the building were a palace, the members of the royal household, but no others, would normally worship the palace-gods at this altar; if this were a temple, people from the city might worship at this altar the god or gods to whom the temple was dedicated. The priests and boys carry wands twined with wool, such as suppliants carried when they went in procession to the temple of a god to pray for relief from some danger or distress. In our own times those participating in processions to churches sometimes carry lighted candles. In the play the priests and the boys group themselves about the altar, lay their wands upon it, and wait, looking towards the door of the stage-building. So far nothing at all has been said. Presently the door of the building is opened and a man comes out, perhaps thirty years old or a little more, dressed as a king. His first words to the crowd about the altar show that this is Thebes, that the building is the king's palace, and that the man himself is the mysterious Oedipus. He expresses surprise that these suppliants have come to his palace as if he were a god and this were his temple. The aged priest replies that, as the king already knows, the city is being destroyed by a frightful pestilence, that the other citizens are pleading for deliverance at the temples and shrines in the two market places of Thebes and elsewhere in the city, that those before him now have been sent as representatives of the people, not because they consider him a god, but because they count him "the first of men," especially when something supernatural is to be dealt with, as when once Oedipus delivered the city from the sphinx. Probably he means that they did not exactly think of him as god, but as something more than man. He exhorts Oedipus to exert all his power again to save the city. The king answers that he is well aware of the pestilence and will do everything he can; already he has sent his wife's brother, Creon, to Delphi to consult the oracle there, and he expects his return at any moment now. While he is speaking Creon appears in the passage at the left, and tells that to save the city the pollution which has been brought upon it must be removed by the death or expulsion of the person or persons by whom the former king, Laïus, was killed. Oedipus promises to do everything possible to discover these persons, dismisses the delegation, and sends a messenger to summon the elders of the city. The priests and boys march away through the passage on the right, returning to the town, and after a moment Creon follows them. When all have disappeared, Oedipus reenters the palace, the doors of which are then closed, and the orchestra is left empty again. All the scenes up to this point belong to what the Greeks called the prologue of the play.

After a pause the Theban elders, who constitute the chorus, enter singing. In their song they describe the pestilence, the misery and terror in the city, and implore the gods to deliver the people from the plague. Oedipus appears again from the palace and makes a formal proclamation. He calls upon all who know anything about the death of Laïus to come forward and give information, even if the informant thereby incriminate himself. He lays a curse upon the slayer or slayers of Laïus, and upon all who conceal or befriend the slayers, even upon his own self if he should protect the slayer. The chorus suggests that the prophet, Teiresias, may be able to reveal the truth. Oedipus says that he has already sent

for him, and presently the very old, blind seer is led in by a
boy. Teiresias admits that he knows, but refuses to tell who
the slayer of Laïus is. Oedipus becomes very angry and
actually threatens the holy man with violence. Finally, exasperated by the king, Teiresias says that Oedipus himself
is the slayer. Oedipus accuses the prophet of being in collusion
with Creon, and assumes that the latter has planned to
destroy Oedipus in order that he himself may become king.
Teiresias prophesies that it will soon be discovered not only
that Oedipus killed Laïus, but also that he killed his own
father and married his own mother, Iocasta, and that in
consequence he will be blinded and will go out from Thebes
a beggar, stripped of all his power and glory. Teiresias then
leaves, while the chorus sings an ode, full of foreboding,
but expressing faith in Oedipus still.

Presently Creon comes to protest against the king's ac-
cusation of which he has just heard. Oedipus comes out of
the palace, and there follows a very stormy dialogue in which
the king asserts that Creon is a traitor to his country and
to his king, while Creon defends himself. Creon shows a
good deal of self-restraint and dignity; but Oedipus shows
temper, obstinacy and vindictiveness, and says that he wishes
Creon's death. Of course both men are excited, both are
deeply hurt, Oedipus because he believes that his brother-in-
law and trusted friend has plotted to destroy him, Creon
because he has been falsely accused of most dishonorable
conduct. The conversation is interrupted by the appearance
of Iocasta who, with the support of the elders, persuades
the king to dismiss Creon without ordering his arrest, although Oedipus remains sullen and unconvinced of Creon's
innocence. When Creon has gone, Iocasta asks how the quarrel with her brother arose. Oedipus says that Creon, through
the prophet, has accused him of being the slayer of Laïus.
Iocasta says that prophets and oracles are not always right,

and gives what she believes to be definite proof of this: an
oracle was given to Laïus that he would be killed by his own
son; but Laïus was killed by bandits at a place where three
roads meet, whereas his only child, when three days old, was
mutilated by having a pin thrust through its ankles, and was
exposed on a trackless mountain, where it must have died.
Thus the oracle was not fulfilled. Oedipus is much disquieted
by Iocasta's statement that Laïus was killed where three roads
meet. In answer to his questions she tells him that the place
is in Phocis, where the roads from Delphi and from Daulia
branch from the road from Thebes, and that the time of
Laïus's death was shortly before Oedipus appeared in Thebes.
She describes Laïus's appearance, and says that he was
travelling in a carriage accompanied by a herald and three
other attendants, of whom only one escaped, a thrall of the
king, now employed at some distance from the town. Oedipus
asks that the man be sent for. Iocasta asks why he wishes
to see this person, and Oedipus then tells to her the story of
his life, apparently for the first time — this is one of the
improbabilities in the play. He says that his parents were
Polybus of Corinth and Merope, a "Dorian." When he was
grown, someone at a banquet asserted that he was not really
the son of those whom he supposed to be his parents. When
he asked them they did not give him a direct answer. Therefore he went to Delphi to consult the oracle. But the god,
without answering his question, told him that he would kill
his father and marry his mother. Therefore he was unwilling to return to Corinth and took the road to Thebes.
At a fork in this road he met a person such as Iocasta described, in a carriage, with a herald and other attendants. A
quarrel arose, and he believes that he killed the whole party. If
this person was Laïus, then he, Oedipus, was Laïus's slayer,
and has laid himself under a direful curse. If, however, there
is a survivor of Laïus's party, and if this survivor testifies

that the party was attacked by a band of men, then it was not Laïus whom Oedipus killed, for he was alone at the time of the quarrel. Iocasta is now somewhat frightened and evidently wishes to avoid any further investigation. But Oedipus insists that the surviving attendant be sent for. Then with Iocasta he withdraws into the palace.

After a song by the chorus, Iocasta appears again, alone, with a suppliant's wand and incense. She tells the elders that Oedipus is too much excited by all sorts of fears. Since by counsel she can accomplish nothing, she wishes to appeal to the gods, and at the altar before the palace she makes a short prayer. It is a very moving scene. Just before this Iocasta has been trying to relieve the anxiety and distress of Oedipus. He is alarmed and may be in danger; but his alarm is due chiefly to the response of the Delphic oracle and the prophecy of Teiresias. She humored him and promised to do all that he wishes. She tried to convince him that no mortal has the skill to reveal the future — the chorus previously had expressed the same thought. She said to him: "As for divination, I would not regard it one way or the other." Thus she comforted him and encouraged him. But now, as soon as she could slip away from him, she has come to pray to the gods for help. For his sake she had concealed her own fear and argued against her own beliefs. But all the while she too was afraid.

Immediately after Iocasta's prayer there enters from the left a messenger from Corinth. He tells the queen that Polybus is dead, and that the people of Corinth wish Oedipus to be their king. This also is an improbability in the play, because Oedipus is already king of Thebes, and it could hardly be thought that in the heroic age of Greece the same person could be king of both Thebes and Corinth. However, this is not important to the plot, except in supplying an explanation for the despatch of the messenger and in leading up to the conversation which follows. The messenger thinks that his message will be welcomed because it contains the offer of a kingdom, and he expects a handsome reward. Iocasta thinks that the news is good because it shows that Oedipus did not kill his father, and therefore the prophecy that Oedipus would kill his father and marry his mother was false. She sends in haste for Oedipus, who comes at once and questions the messenger. The messenger says that Polybus has died of sickness and old age. Oedipus is glad that now at least the first part of the prophecy cannot be fulfilled, but says that he still fears to return to Corinth lest he fulfill the second part. It was on account of the oracle given to him at Delphi that he never came home again. The messenger says that he could have freed him from that anxiety long ago, for Oedipus was not the son of Polybus and Merope at all. He, the messenger himself, had brought Oedipus, an infant with mutilated ankles, to the king and queen of Corinth who were childless. The messenger had received the child on Mt. Cithaeron from another shepherd who was said to be a servant of Laïus. The elders think this may be the man for whom the king has already sent. By this time Iocasta understands all the horrible facts. She tries to stop the inquiry, and, failing to do so, rushes into the palace overwhelmed with shame and grief. Oedipus impetuously assumes that she fears that he will be shown to be a slave's son; but he is determined to find out at any cost who his parents were. The chorus sings a short ode, almost gay in tone, affording a moment's relief from the tension; the elders express pleasure in the thought that Oedipus will be found to be a native Theban, not a foreign-born adventurer, and suggest that perhaps his parents were divine. Soon the Theban shepherd is brought in, the man who was with Laïus when Laïus was killed. He is not asked about the killing. It seems to be assumed that his story of an attack by a band of men was

false, told only to avoid the disgrace of having been one
of five overcome by a single man. It seems to be assumed
also that he recognized Oedipus when the latter arrived at
Thebes and became king, and that for this reason he asked
to be sent away from the city. Nothing is said now about all
this. Confronted with the Corinthian messenger who recognizes him, reluctantly, under threat of torture, he admits
that he did give the baby to this Corinthian, that the child
was said to be the son of Laïus, and that the queen herself
gave the child to him to expose on the mountain because it
had been foretold that this child would kill his father. So
the whole truth is made known. Oedipus goes into the palace,
crushed. The elders sing one of the saddest, most touching
odes in all literature.

Presently a house servant comes out of the palace and
tells what has happened indoors. Iocasta, when she rushed in,
went at once to her bed chamber, and there, calling out the
name of Laïus, mourned over her first-born child, who in
ignorance killed his father, and became the father of her
other children. Then she hung herself. Oedipus, rushing in
soon afterwards, broke down the door of the bedroom and
found the body of his wife and mother. He took the body
down and laid it upon the ground. Then, bending over the
body, he drew out the heavy gold brooches which held her
dress over her shoulders, and with these brooches he blinded
himself, saying that his eyes should no longer see the horrors
which he was suffering and committing. Now he is calling
for someone to open the palace door and lead him forth and
away from Thebes, to free his house — and the city — from
the curse.

The blinded Oedipus is then led out, his face streaming
with blood, and there follows a most affecting scene in which
the king and the elders lament together. Creon appears, and
takes charge of the situation. He suggests that Oedipus be

taken indoors again. Oedipus begs Creon to send him out of
the country. Creon replies that in such a case as this he must
await divine instructions. Oedipus asks Creon to arrange a
proper burial for the queen's body, and to permit him to
return to Mt. Cithaeron, the place which his parents had
once chosen for his death. However, he says, he knows that
neither sickness nor anything else can destroy him, but that
some more dreadful end is in store for him. He also begs
Creon to care for his daughters and provide suitable mar-
riages for them; his two sons will soon be men and will be
able to take care of themselves. The two girls are brought
out, and Oedipus, thanking Creon for his thoughtfulness and
kindness in arranging for this last interview, caresses his
daughters and bids them farewell. Oedipus, and soon afterwards the two girls are led back into the palace. Creon withdraws, the elders and all others walk away.

It is an outstanding fact that in the *Oedipus Tyrannus* of
Sophocles the existence of a pollution, caused by the killing
of a father by his son and by the marriage of that son with
his own mother, preceded the situation with which the play
begins, and lies outside of the plot. Such things are of course
possible in the given circumstances. The notion that a pollution involving the gravest consequences may result from acts
committed without any improper motive, or any consciousness
that there was anything improper in the acts themselves, is
common to most, if not to all primitive peoples, and is met
frequently in ancient literature. The Greeks of Sophocles
time had not entirely outgrown this notion.

In the story of Oedipus, as it was dramatized by Sophocles,
it is evident that the pollution was not due to any deliberate
sin on the part of Oedipus himself or of the people of
Thebes. It could not be regarded as a sin or a fault in
Oedipus that he, while travelling, killed in a fair fight another

man who had provoked a quarrel, or that afterwards, at the invitation of the Thebans, he married the widowed queen and became king. It may be thought that Oedipus should have discovered who his parents were, that the Thebans should have found out who killed Laïus. But it seems to me that the faults of Oedipus and the Thebans, if they were really faults, were at most contributory to the calamity. And it must be remembered that Oedipus tried in every way possible for him to learn who his parents were. The king and queen of Corinth, who must have known, if anybody knew, refused to tell him. He then consulted the oracle of Delphi as the surest way. The oracle refused to tell him, but gave him such other information that he was afraid to return to Corinth even to ask further questions. What else could he have done? There was nothing else. I think that the oracle meant that the pollution would occur whatever Oedipus or the Thebans might try to do.

Or were these calamities the consequence of sins committed by other and perhaps unknown persons? Then was the punishment for the sins of others laid upon these innocent ones, Oedipus and the people of Thebes? That explanation was proposed by some later Greeks, but there is no hint of it in Sophocles.

Oedipus in one place (lines 813 *ff.*), speaking of his misfortune if it should prove true that Laïus was the man he killed, so that he will then be under the curse which he himself pronounced against the man who killed Laïus, and must leave Thebes and all he loves, as once he fled from his old home in Corinth, leaving all he loved there, in order not to become the slayer of his father and the husband of his mother, says: "Am I then vile? Am I not all accursed? . . . Would one not rightly say that these things have been brought upon me by a cruel demon?" And later, when the full catastrophe has fallen, he says (lines 1329 *f.*): "It was Apollo who brought all these evil experiences upon me." But I do not think that Oedipus really believes either of these things, or that Sophocles intended to suggest that either a malignant devil or some god such as Apollo was the cause of these shocking occurrences. I do not think that any of Sophocles' audience would have accepted that.

Or was it chance? That, I think, would satisfy nobody.

Was it then fate? Did fate, in the sense of an inscrutable power, superior to gods and men, a power which nothing can resist and no one can comprehend, cause this pollution with all its consequences to fall upon persons innocent of conscious sin? What a monstrous and repulsive doctrine that would be! If Sophocles, or the Greeks of his time, were so primitive as to hold such a belief, how were they then great?

There is no more of fate as an inscrutable, resistless, arbitrary power in what remains of ancient Greek tragedy than in our own everyday thought and speech. The ancient Greeks were no more fatalists than we are. To them fate was a word for whatever actually happened. This might be known beforehand, e.g. to the gods, and might even be revealed to men through prophecy or oracles. But when it happened, it happened by the will of the gods or by man's own choice. The common opinion that the ancient Greeks differed from us in their belief in fate is in my judgment wholly without foundation. There is no fate (in the usual sense) in Greek tragedy.

To me it seems clear that Sophocles in his *Oedipus Tyrannus* presents the view that the pollution could not have been avoided by the people who suffered in consequence of it. The fact of the pollution is given in the premises. But the cause of the pollution is not explained. It was known beforehand that certain people would act as they did act. This knowledge was revealed by an oracle. But the oracle did not cause these people to act as they did, nor did the gods cause the events through the oracle. The story which Sophocles chose as the subject of his play gives rise to a problem of the greatest magnitude. But Sophocles made no attempt to solve this problem. The story was enough for him, and out of it he made a magnificent drama.

The consequences of the pollution might have been the total destruction of the people of Thebes. In this play it is permitted by the grace of the gods that the consequences of the pollution were finally laid upon the innocent head of Oedipus alone, and thus the remaining Thebans were absolved. That is emphasized particularly in the ending of Seneca's *Oedipus,* which was derived chiefly from Sophocles. If so, then is there here perhaps some analogy to the old Hebrew idea of the scapegoat, or to the Christian doctrine of the vicarious atonement? Personally, I do not think that there was any such idea in Sophocles' mind. The vision of Oedipus the Great, now completely crushed, leaving everything behind, bearing on himself the burden of the horrors which he had unwittingly caused, is tragic and affecting enough to have delighted the artistic soul of Sophocles. It seems to me that he took the story as he found it, because it was most suitable for a tragic drama, and he presented it effectively, without reflection on its implications.

Whatever inner meaning this play may have, or doctrine, it portrays most vividly, in a series of powerful and moving scenes, the greatest character in Greek fiction.

The chief and most outstanding quality in Oedipus is courage, the most necessary quality in facing the inevitable, universal, disciplinary vicissitudes of human life, the common burden of our race.

X

THE *PHILOCTETES* OF SOPHOCLES

THE *Philoctetes* of Sophocles, like Aeschylus's *Eumenides*, is a tragedy without a death and with a happy ending. It is also without a woman. In it a young person named Neoptolemus, the son of Achilles, is changed from a boy to a man in a single day. An astonishing transformation!

With this story there is united in the plot the story of another man, Philoctetes, who started out with the Greek expedition against Troy, but, because he was bitten by some sort of miraculous serpent and was incapacitated, became an offensive and dangerous companion, was deserted by his associates and marooned on the island of Lemnos, where for ten years he suffered frequently recurring attacks of pain and delirium, and nursed his hatred of the Greeks, especially Agamemnon and Odysseus. One thing, however, Philoctetes had which saved him from actual starvation and made him still formidable: that was the bow of Heracles which never missed.

Two other ancient dramas based on these legends are known, one by Aeschylus and one by Euripides. Sophocles' play was the latest of the three, and was produced near the end of its author's very long life, probably in 409 B.C. That date falls between the recall of Alcibiades in 411 and his return to Athens in 407 B.C. Some people see a reflection of Alcibiades in Philoctetes, and of Thrasybulus in Neoptolemus.

Jebb, in his introduction to Sophocles' play has given all one needs to know about the legends involved. The epic version is mentioned in *Iliad* II, 716-28 and in *Odyssey* III, 190 and VIII, 219 *f*. It was contained in the *Cypria,* assigned to Stasinus of Cyprus, in the *Little Iliad,* assigned to Lesches of Mitylene, and in the *Sack of Troy,* assigned to Arctinus

of Miletus, which are known chiefly from the summaries of
their contents given in Proclus's *Chrestomathia,* assigned
to the second century after Christ and partly preserved in
Proclus's *Bibliotheca* 239 and in the introduction to the
scholia on the *Iliad* in Codex Venetus A. According to this
version, Philoctetes was bitten by the snake on Tenedos or
on Chryse, and abandoned on Lemnos. Calchas, the prophet
of the Greeks, after years of unsuccessful war, told them
that they must obtain certain knowledge possessed only by
the Trojan Helenus, a son of Priam and also a prophet.
Helenus was captured by Odysseus, and told the Greeks that
they could take the city only if they brought Neoptolemus
from Scyros and Philoctetes with his bow from Lemnos.
Odysseus was sent to fetch Neoptolemus, and Diomed to
fetch Philoctetes. Thereupon, Philoctetes was healed by
Machaon, the physician of the Greek host, and killed Paris in
single combat, Neoptolemus killed Priam, and both were
among the leaders of the Greeks in the capture of Troy.

The dramas of Aeschylus and of Euripides dealing with
these legends have been lost. But Dion of Prusa, called
Chrysostom, the Golden-Mouthed, who was born about the
middle of the first century after Christ and died early in the
second century, discussed all three plays about Philoctetes
by Aeschylus, Euripides and Sophocles, comparing each with
the others, in one of his lectures, and gave a paraphrase of
the opening scene of Euripides' play in another. These lectures
of Dion (*Or.* LII and LIX) are extant. From them, and
from a few quotations or "fragments," we learn something
about the lost plays. Aeschylus made Odysseus — of all
persons the most unsuitable — bring Philoctetes from Lemnos. In this play Philoctetes did not recognize Odysseus,
although he believed that Odysseus and Agamemnon were
chiefly responsible for his ruthless treatment by the Greeks,
and hated these two leaders especially. He was deceived by

Odysseus's story that both Agamemnon and Odysseus were dead, and that the Greek host was in great danger. Odysseus got possession of the bow, probably while Philoctetes was having one of his attacks of pain, and the two left for Troy together. The chorus was composed of Lemnians, so that evidently Lemnos was not regarded as uninhabited. In the *Philoctetes* of Euripides, which is said to have belonged to the same tetralogy as the Medea and to have been produced in 431 B.C., Odysseus and Diomed together came for Philoctetes. Odysseus was afraid, but was encouraged by Athena. He was not recognized, and claimed to be a fugitive from the injustice of the Greek leaders. He asked Philoctetes to protect him, and thus won the sympathy and confidence of the injured man. He also said that an embassy from the Trojans was on the way to ask Philoctetes to join their cause, and presently the Trojan embassy appeared. After a dramatic debate, Philoctetes was finally persuaded to support the Greeks. Probably he then had a seizure, and Diomed got the bow. Odysseus was helped by Actor, a Lemnian, friendly to Philoctetes. The chorus was composed of Lemnians. Thus in this play also Lemnos was considered an inhabited island.

Sophocles' play is fundamentally different. The introduction of Neoptolemus in the plot transfers the chief interest to him. Here, at the very beginning, it is made evident that Odysseus alone has been sent, first to bring Neoptolemus from Scyros, and then to get Philoctetes and his bow. The first part of his mission, of course, presented no difficulty at all. In those days when fighting and knight-errantry were the most glamorous occupations of the nobles, a young prince would have been immensely flattered to have a warrior, his father's friend and one of the most famous heroes of his time, seek him out, would have been immensely pleased to be asked to join the heroes and take a leading part in the capture of a great city for which the Greeks had been fighting vainly for more than nine years. He needed no persuasion to come along. Now these two together have arrived at Lemnos to undertake the difficult and dangerous part of Odysseus's task. The island is uninhabited, and the chorus, which enters a little later, is composed of sailors, apparently from a ship under Neoptolemus's command. Somewhere on the island is a madman, crazed by years of hardship and pain, and in his hands is the bow of Heracles which never missed its aim. The cave where the man lives is soon found, and to it there leads a single narrow path through the rocks. To walk up that path, if Philoctetes is at the head of it, is like going through a narrow passage in the face of a maniac, armed with a machine gun, who hates his former associates, Odysseus most of all. In the play the stage-building seems to have been simply ignored, or else its opened door must have been made to suggest the entrance to a cave.

Neoptolemus is a young man about eighteen years old, who so far has lived on the quiet island of Scyros. Why he lived there instead of living at his father's capital in Phthia no one knows. His character has not been developed by any active contact with the world. He is very eager to enter the Greek service and to prove his worth; he is full of admiration and respect for the older man, the famous hero, anxious to obey his orders, ready to receive his first assignment. Odysseus tells him that he himself cannot meet Philoctetes openly. Neoptolemus must go alone, must make acquaintance with the madman, must deceive him with a lie and win his confidence. He must admit that he is Achilles' son, but must say that he is on his way home from Troy, that he has abandoned the Greek cause and now hates the Greek leaders because, when his father was killed, they slighted him by giving his father's arms to crafty Odysseus. Then, somehow, he must come close to Philoctetes and, if possible, get possession of the bow. The rest will be easy. At first the boy is unwilling to adopt this plan, which seems to him dishonorable; he would prefer to risk an honest approach to Philoctetes, and, if necessary, a fair fight. The worldly-wise Odysseus persuades him by very subtle arguments and inducements to do what the youth believes to be wrong and contemptible.

Neoptolemus is influenced by the following considerations.

1. His respect for the older man, already known to him as one of the greatest warriors of his time, and by his unwillingness to refuse the first task laid upon him by his father's comrades.

2. His fear that if he does refuse he will be thought young and foolish.

3. The apparent impossibility of succeeding otherwise.

4. The argument that the end will justify the means.

5. The temptation to appear mature and brave. Odysseus has said to him: "Now lend thyself to me for one small, shameless part of a day, and then for the rest of time be called the most upright of all mortals."

The young man stifles his scruples and his sense of honor. He undertakes the dangerous task. He meets Philoctetes and engages him in conversation without being attacked. The lie succeeds, and he wins the man's confidence. Philoctetes tells his story and describes his hardships and misery on this barren, deserted island. Neoptolemus continues his tale, which is partly true, but essentially false. He says that when his father was killed, Odysseus and Phoenix, his father's tutor, brought him to Troy to take his father's place, but when he arrived there the leaders refused to give him his father's arms, which they had awarded to Odysseus. The latter was particularly offensive. Consequently Neoptolemus has sailed for home and is now on his way. Philoctetes says that he and Neoptolemus alike have a grievance against Odysseus. He asks about the other Greek chieftains. Ajax is dead also. Nestor has troubles of his own now since the death of his son,

Antilochus. Patroclus is dead. Thersites, the opponent of
Odysseus, is still alive, but Neoptolemus did not see him.
Rocky Scyros is pleasant enough for him, and he pretends to
be ready to start on at once. Philoctetes earnestly begs to be
taken along. The chorus, sailors from Neoptolemus's ship, aid
in the deception by seeming to urge their commander to take
the wounded man with them. Neoptolemus, feigning hesitation, consents. Just then, to make sure that Philoctetes will
embark on the ship of his own accord, an attendant of
Neoptolemus disguised as a merchant is sent by Odysseus
with another false story. He says that he is on his way from
Troy to Peparethos and, happening to anchor off this coast,
saw another ship there. Learning that it belongs to
Neoptolemus, he has come with news for which he hopes to
be rewarded. Phoenix and the sons of Theseus have started in
pursuit of Neoptolemus himself, while Odysseus and Diomed
have set out to get Philoctetes, by force if necessary. In explanation he says that Helenus has told them that the Greeks
would never capture Troy unless they have Philoctetes with
them. This story makes Philoctetes all the more eager to go
with Neoptolemus. But, before they can leave, the wounded
man feels another seizure coming on. He begs the young
prince, whom he believes to be his friend and protector, not
to leave him, and gives his bow to Neoptolemus, lest those
who are coming to capture him get the bow and thus rob him
of his only means of defense. Then Philoctetes becomes delirious and violent, but is tended by Neoptolemus until at last
he falls exhausted and unconscious. The chorus suggests that
they can now sail with the bow, leaving the sick man behind,
but Neoptolemus reminds them that their orders are to bring
the man himself.

When Philoctetes has recovered sufficiently he, with
Neoptolemus and the sailors, starts out for the ship,
Neoptolemus carrying the bow, and the victim himself urging

all possible haste in the belief that he is being taken back to Greece. So Odysseus's plan has been successful, and the dangerous task has been accomplished. But in carrying out this plan the character of Neoptolemus has been matured, his attitude towards the deception of Philoctetes changed by the following steps.

1. At first he was intoxicated by his success in playing his exciting rôle.

2. He was flattered by the equality with which Philoctetes treated him — Odysseus had treated him as a boy — and by the friendship which Philoctetes offered him.

3. He was even praised by Philoctetes.

4. At the same time his sympathy for Philoctetes has been developed. This sympathy was first awakened by his imagining the plight of the injured warrior while talking with his own men, the chorus, before Philoctetes appeared. It was perhaps increased by thinking of his own imaginary injury, which was part of the lie. It was further increased by Philoctetes' own account of his experiences. It became overpowering when he witnessed Philoctetes' actual suffering.

5. With this sympathy was joined the satisfaction of protecting and helping a most pitiable person in great distress, developed while he was nursing Philoctetes in the latter's agony.

6. Success brought reaction and remorse.

7. Perhaps also Philoctetes' violent denunciation of both Neoptolemus and Odysseus, when finally told the truth, added something to Neoptolemus's appreciation of his own treachery.

Before they have gone far, the change which has been taking place in Neoptolemus reaches its crisis. The young man stops and tells his victim that he has deceived him, that he is not taking him home but is taking him to Troy, and that all this while he has been acting on the instructions of Odysseus, who is now on the island waiting for them both. Philoctetes is of course intensely angry. Neoptolemus tries to convince him that the deception was for the victim's own good, that he may be saved from his present hardships and may participate in the capture of Troy. But the sufferer is not appeased, and demands that his bow be given back at once. Neoptolemus wavers, until Odysseus, appearing suddenly, asks for the bow. Philoctetes at once recognizes this his most hated enemy, and turns upon him all his pent-up bitterness and rage. Odysseus is perfectly cold and ruthless. He first orders the sailors to seize the now helpless warrior; but then, seeming to alter his plan, he orders the sailors to release their captive and directs Neoptolemus to accompany him to the ship, leaving Philoctetes to perish without his bow; he asserts that he himself can wield the bow of Heracles as well as anyone. Neoptolemus complies, but first tells his men to stay with Philoctetes a while longer, in the hope that the latter will change his mind.

Left alone with the sufferer, the chorus reasons with him, not without some sympathy for him, tries to defend Odysseus and to show that no course is open to Philoctetes but to submit. But the latter does not relent. He complains bitterly of his sufferings, of the injustice and cruelty with which he has been treated, and finally of the loss of his bow. He tells the sailors to leave him alone, then asks them for a weapon with which to end his life. In his bitterness he expresses the hope that both Troy and all the host encamped about it will perish. Just then Neoptolemus returns, followed by Odysseus. The former says that he is going to return the bow to its owner. The latter forbids this; he first argues, then, laying his hand upon his sword, commands the young man to give the bow to him. It must be remembered that Odysseus was now at his prime, physically as well as in other ways,

a soldier trained and hardened by long years of war. Since
Achilles was now dead, and Ajax, and Hector, it may be
assumed that at the moment Odysseus was the greatest, the
most powerful fighting man in all the world. Neoptolemus
was still a boy. He had never fought anybody. He had no
chance against Odysseus — no chance at all. And yet, when
this famous champion, with a threat of fighting, ordered the
new recruit to give the bow to him, the untried soldier refused
to do it, and he did not do it. The boy had become a man.

Odysseus withdraws for a moment, but reappears when
Neoptolemus is about to give the bow back to Philoctetes. In
vain Odysseus forbids the return of the bow, then threatens
to carry off Philoctetes by force. Philoctetes, now armed
again, aims an arrow at Odysseus, but is prevented by
Neoptolemus from shooting. Odysseus then goes away, and
is not seen again. Neoptolemus, now really a friend, gently
reproves Philoctetes for his bitterness and obstinacy, appeals
to his ambition, and urges him to go willingly to Troy, there
to be healed of his malady and to share in the victory. The
injured man is moved by this plea, but he cannot bring himself to yield. He asks how eyes that have seen all his sufferings
can endure to see him consorting with the sons of Atreus
or with the accursed Odysseus. Yet in his next sentence he
says that it is not resentment for past injuries which vexes
him, but his belief that further injustice will be done to
Neoptolemus and himself by the Greek chieftains. He will
not go to Troy. He recalls the promise made by Neoptolemus
to take him home. At last Neoptolemus agrees to keep this
promise, though he may incur punishment from the Greeks
thereby. They start for the ship, but are stopped by the god
Heracles himself, who appears to them and tells them that
they shall go to the besieged city, where Philoctetes will be
healed and where glory awaits them both. Philoctetes cannot
disobey the divine command, and with his bow, in company

with Neoptolemus and Neoptolemus's sailors, he sets out
again for Troy.

I do not think that the restitution of the miraculous bow
to Philoctetes was an impulsive, quixotic act. Nor do I think
that at the moment any shrewd calculation affected the action
of Neoptolemus, for example, that he could get the bow back
later by persuasion if, by returning it now, he won again the
confidence and gratitude of its owner, or that without
Philoctetes himself the bow would be enough — the prophet
had said "Philoctetes *and* the bow." Neoptolemus seems
to me far too sincere and naïve for anything like that. I
think Neoptolemus returned the bow simply because genuine
sympathy for Philoctetes and a sense of justice outweighed
the arguments and influence of Odysseus, and brought
Neoptolemus again to his original opinion that the treachery
proposed by Odysseus was dishonorable.

I do not suppose that anyone in the ancient world or now
could fail to have a good deal of liking and enthusiasm for
this young Neoptolemus. In fact it throws some light on the
civilization of the ancient Greeks that such a person as
Neoptolemus could be conceived in the fifth century B.C.
But it is not at all clear that Neoptolemus was wrong at first
in deceiving Philoctetes, and thus getting possession of the
bow and the man treacherously. For this was a time of war,
and Neoptolemus a soldier now in active service. It seems
to me certain that he did wrong in returning the bow, however
noble his purpose. He could not and did not thereby put the
matter back where it was before. Philoctetes now knew the
facts. When Neoptolemus returned the bow which never
missed to an enemy in possession of all the facts, he did a
positive injury to his own associates. From the consequences
of this injury they were saved only by the intervention of
a god.

Neoptolemus's act in restoring the bow presented a serious problem to Philoctetes, whether he should accept restoration to the world to which he naturally belonged, the healing of his wound, the curing of his disease, and honor and glory and all that, or indulge his hatred, take revenge upon his faithless friends at the expense of the continuation of his own sufferings and misery. If he had been a Christian, I suppose he should have forgiven those who had injured him and left vengeance to God. Certainly in so doing he would have repaid evil with good to the Greeks who had ill treated him. Would he have done good thereby to the poor Trojans who had not injured him? In that age was he not free to decide that question as he chose?

The problem presented to Neoptolemus was a moral problem. It seems to me a very hard problem. Who can say what it is right to do in such circumstances? Similar situations may arise for any of us at any time. Who can say whether a spy in war is justified morally in doing what he does? Sophocles, as usual, attempts no solution. That is the reason why, at the end, he brings in Heracles to provide by fiat a way out of an impasse.

XI

THE *ALCESTIS* OF EURIPIDES

Like Sophocles' *Philoctetes*, the *Alcetis* of Euripides, which is believed to be nearly thirty years the earlier, presents the development of a man's character in a single day. But there is this difference. The previous immaturity of Neoptolemus in the *Philoctetes* was due to his youth. Admetus, in the *Alcestis,* is a grown man, married, with two children old enough to walk and talk. He has been a ruling king for some time, though his parents are still alive. His immaturity is due to the fact that his life so far has been sheltered and easy. He has had no serious difficulties to overcome, no crises to face, no hardships, sufferings, disappointments, or sorrows to endure. Thus when a crisis does confront him he is unprepared, cowardly, and self-centered. Yet he emerges at the end of this crowded day humbled, purified and strong.

In a brief notice of this play, by some unknown Greek author, it is said that "the drama was made seventeenth" — probably that means that it was the seventeenth in some list or collection of Euripides' works — and that "it was produced when Glaucinus was archon," i.e. in 438 B.C. If Euripides was really born in 480 B.C., as tradition has it, then he was forty-two years old when he produced this play. This has a certain importance, for there is a tradition that Euripides was married twice. There were stories that both of his wives were unfaithful to him, but these stories conflict with information about the poet which seems more reliable, and probably they were merely slanderous or else deductions from the false assumption that this dramatist was a woman-hater. Consequently, it has been suggested that the *Alcestis* reflects to some extent the personal experience of its author. For example, Gilbert Norwood, who is inclined to think this play much earlier than the date commonly assigned to it, says

(*Greek Tragedy,* 1920, p. 192, n.1) : "To me it reads essentially like the work of a young but highly-gifted playwright
who has recently lost his wife." The notice referred to says
also that in the contest on this occasion "Sophocles was first,
Euripides second with the *Cretan Women, Alcmaeon in
Psophis, Telephus,* and *Alcestis,*" and that the last of these
was "somewhat like a satyr-play," doubtless meaning that
one of the characters, Heracles, is a somewhat comic figure,
like the persons in a satyr-play — in one scene Heracles appears half-drunk, and makes fun of the servant who has
been ordered to provide for his entertainment. Moreover, the
Alcestis, though really a tragedy in the ancient Greek sense,
was apparently the fourth member of a tetralogy, which
would normally be a satyr-play.

The legend on which the play is based was probably an old
one before Euripides' time. Zeus had killed Apollo's son
Asclepius with his thunderbolt. Therefore Apollo killed the
Cyclopes who made the bolt. In punishment Zeus compelled
Apollo, though a god, to serve for a year in the household
of Admetus, king of Pherae in Thessaly. While a servant
there Apollo became fond of Admetus and all his house. He
persuaded the three Fates that when the time came for Admetus to die his life would be spared if someone else died
for him. No one was willing to give his life for the king's,
except the king's own wife, Alcestis : she consented. Alcestis
died and was buried. But Heracles, who happened to be visit-
ing Admetus just at this time, sought out Death, defeated
him, and brought back Alcestis from the grave.

The play opens with the appearance of Apollo, who comes
out of the palace, where for some unexplained reason he has
been making a short visit. Death arrives and converses angrily
with Apollo, who then withdraws while Death enters the
palace. Next the chorus appears, composed of citizens of
Pherae; they know that the queen is about to die. A maid

comes out of the palace in tears and tells what is happening within. The maid and the chorus discuss the situation; they make clear their admiration for Alcestis and their regret that Admetus is allowing her to die for him, but express their affection for both. Presently Admetus comes out of the palace with Alcestis, followed by their two children, the older one apparently a little boy, the younger a girl (lines 165 *f.*, 311 *ff.*, 406 *ff.*). She asks her husband not to marry again, and to devote himself faithfully to bringing up their children. And Admetus gives his promise. Throughout this rather long scene Alcestis appears sad, composed and practical; but Admetus is shallow and emotional, almost hysterical. It seems clear that each loves the other. But evidently she appreciates his faults. She shows towards him something like the understanding and protectiveness of a mother dealing with her child. It is noticeable that she gives only practical reasons for dying in his stead, never alluding to love on her part or devotion to him for his own sake. Admetus is not naturally a coward, nor is he strictly selfish. He is too self-centered to be selfish, to be conscious of a conflict of interest between himself and anyone else. Apparently it seemed to him natural that everyone should be willing to sacrifice anything, even life itself if necessary, for him — everyone always had. Perhaps he thought when the bargain with the Fates was made that the time of payment was far off; something might intervene. Or perhaps he did not think about it very much at all. So he accepted Alcestis's offer. Such a thing could not really happen. Now it has happened, and he cannot bear it. Yet even now he seems more concerned about his own bereavement than about her.

Alcestis dies, the children are led away, and Admetus, after giving in dignified sadness orders for the funeral and for a period of twelve months' mourning throughout the kingdom,

withdraws into the palace, while the chorus sings an ode in
praise of the devoted queen.

Then Heracles enters, alone, masterful, in high spirits,
somewhat boisterous. He is on his way to get the steeds of
the Thracian Diomed, sent by Eurystheus the king of Tiryns,
whom he has to serve. This was one of the twelve "labors"
of Heracles. The chorus tells him that these horses are extremely dangerous; they attack and devour men. But the
hero is not dismayed; this will be only one more fight,
one more danger to be overcome. Robert Browning, in his
Balaustion's Adventure, gives in narrative form the story of
the *Alcestis,* enlarging and interpreting some of the scenes.
This poem has been justly described as a poet's interpretation of a poet. Browning dwells at some length on the effect
of Heracles' appearance when the preceding episodes and the
futile lamentation of the chorus have displayed the weakness
and the fecklessness of all concerned.

A great voice —
"My hosts here!" Oh, the thrill that ran through us!
Never was aught so good and opportune
As that great interrupting voice! For see!
Here maundered this dispirited old age
Before the palace ....
Then ....
Sudden into the midst of sorrow, leapt
Along with the gay cheer of that great voice,
Hope, joy, salvation: Herakles was here!

....
Clearly there was no telling such an one
How, when their monarch tried who loved him more
Than he loved them and found they loved, as he,
Each man, himself, and held, no otherwise,
That, of all evils in the world, the worst

Was — being forced to die, whate'er death gain:
How all this selfishness in him and them
Caused certain sorrow which they sang about —
I think that Herakles, who held his life
Out on his hand, for any man to take —
I think his laugh had marred their threnody.

While Heracles is talking with the chorus Admetus comes
out again. He welcomes Heracles as his friend and guest. He
is dressed in mourning and very sad. He says that he must
hold a funeral today, but conceals the fact that it is Alcestis
who has died. Heracles proposes to withdraw, but Admetus
will not let him go, and directs a servant to provide for the
visitor's needs. The servant conducts Heracles into the palace.
The leader of the chorus protests against entertaining an
outsider at this time; but the king asks whether men would
praise him more if he turned away a guest. Besides, he says,
he may need such a friend himself if he should ever have
occasion to visit Argos. His own house has never been inhos-
pitable; he does not wish it to be so now. Evidently this last
is his real reason.

When Admetus has gone into the palace again, the chorus
sings an ode in praise of hospitality, and of this royal family
with which even the god Apollo once dwelt happily. The
singing of this ode also implies the passing of a certain un-
specified amount of time. Presently the doors of the palace are
opened and Admetus comes out with the rest of his household, some of them bearing the body of the queen. A funeral
procession is formed; but when it is ready to start for the
grave, Pheres, the former king and Admetus's father, appears, bringing gifts for the burial. Admetus faces him
angrily. He calls his father and his mother cowards, and
curses them both. He will be a son to them no longer. He
refuses their gifts to the dead, and orders his father away.

These parents of his — they are already old, they have already enjoyed most of what life can give, now they have refused to sacrifice the little that is left of life for them to save their son, still a young man, from death. By their refusal they have made it necessary for Alcestis to sacrifice her life. The father answers justly, though deeply incensed. He begot Admetus to be the master of their house; he brought him up. Admetus is now the king and will soon inherit all his father's broad estates. He has had everything he had any right to expect. There was no obligation on his parents to die for him. Admetus himself has been the coward and has caused Alcestis's death. Thus they wrangle, until Pheres leaves in a rage. Of course Admetus is in a highly emotional state. His unreasonable and violent temper, his momentary lack of affection and respect for his parents, his efforts to lay all the blame on them and others, show that he is beginning to be conscious that he himself is at fault. When his father has gone, a reaction sets in. Sorrow for his bereavement comes over him, and perhaps the beginning of conscious regret and shame that he has not played a nobler part.

The funeral procession moves away, and with it go all the household and those present outside the palace. The orchestra is empty again; no one is left behind except the servant who was told to remain and to entertain the visitor. The servant comes out and, in soliloquy, complains bitterly of the guest's inconsiderate behavior and boisterous merrymaking at such a time as this. Heracles then appears, partly intoxicated, and says to the servant: You there, what makes you look so solemn and pensive? Stop this silly grieving and have a drink! But suddenly he becomes suspicious, demands to know who has died, and learns that it was the queen herself. That sobers him instantly. He asks where she is being buried, and goes off at once, just as he is, to fight with Death and bring back Alcestis from the grave.

Time passes and Admetus returns with the funeral procession. The sight of the empty house completes his realization of his sorrow, and his appreciation of the baseness of his own behavior. He says: "Friends . . . I have learned my lesson only now. How shall I enter into this my home?" The chorus tries to comfort him, but their words are empty. Then Heracles reappears, and with him a woman, veiled, a young woman evidently, who does not speak, but whose figure and carriage are strangely like hers who just now was buried. Heracles reproves the king for concealing his bereavement, for allowing a guest to make merry in a house of mourning, for refusing to allow his friend to share his sorrow. This friend has found out the truth from others. However, he would not grieve the king further now. He himself is on his way to get the Thracian steeds when he has fought their master for them. He has turned back to the palace only to bring this woman, the prize of a mighty struggle, set for all men, a contest which he has won just now at the risk of his own life. He cannot take the woman with him to Thrace. His friend, the king, must take care of her until he himself returns. Should he not come again, he gives her to this friend to keep. Perhaps in time even the stricken king will thank him. Admetus excuses himself for having concealed his loss, but begs Heracles not to leave the woman with him. He cannot bear to see her, because she reminds him so poignantly of his dead wife. She would not be safe except in the queen's own chamber. He cannot allow her there — he could not endure that. His people would not tolerate it. It would be disloyal to his wife. He will never marry again; he has promised. Heracles still insists, and at last takes off the veil, but Admetus will not look at the woman. Finally, most reluctantly, Admetus consents, looks, and sees that the woman is Alcestis. But she, who has risen from the dead, cannot speak until the third day has come.

The contrast between Heracles and Admetus sharply il-
luminates the weakness of the latter's character. Yet Admetus
is by no means without certain lovable qualities. Heracles
was his friend. Apollo loved him, and I think his wife loved
him too. His servants and his people seem to have been fond
of him, though they regretted his weakness and self-centered-
ness. He shows a good deal of dignity (except in the death
scene), a well-bred courtesy in receiving Heracles, some
masterfulness in arranging for the entertainment of his
guest and for the funeral. At the end he makes an honest
confession of his faults and shows humility, repentance, genuine affection, and gratitude. But when he was put to the
test, his character had been undeveloped.

In this play the experiences which bring Admetus to an
understanding of himself, and which effect a change in him,
are these.

1. The shock of Alcestis's death, and his grief at her loss,
which I believe genuine in spite of his mawkish sentimentality.

2. The realization that those about him condemn him, and
that the whole world will soon despise him. He cares a good
deal about what others think of him.

3. Some appreciation of the manliness of Heracles, in
spite of all that hero's coarseness.

4. The necessity of ordering the funeral, and of providing
in some way for the life of his children and of himself.

5. The talk with his father, who bluntly points out his
faults.

6. The funeral itself and the burial.

7. Lastly and chiefly, the return to the empty house.

No one can help wondering whether the change in Admetus
was permanent. Only a sufficient lapse of time could make
possible a convincing demonstration of such a change, and
in the ancient Greek theater, without a curtain and with the

traditional conventions of the ancient drama, the assumption of such a lapse of time was impossible. It is fair to observe, however, that one can hardly imagine a scene, following immediately upon the preceding scenes, which would give evidence of the genuineness of a change in Admetus more convincingly than the scene with which Euripides ends this play.

It is said sometimes that the Greek tragedies are not very interesting because all or most of them are based on "fairy stories." For example, such things as happen in the *Alcestis* do not happen in real life. But the legends on which the ancient tragedies were based are often typical of possible, if not common, human experiences, though sometimes exaggerated or allegorized. Some years ago a story appeared in a popular magazine. It was the story of a young professor in a small college, who had a wife, two small children, and a very small salary. The only hope of getting a better income seemed to him to be to finish the research on which he was engaged, write a book about it, and so attract attention and obtain a more lucrative position. But the wife became ill, and the doctor said that she must go to some other place. The professor said he could not leave his work. The wife said she knew it was not necessary for her to go away; she would be all right. But she grew worse. Friends intervened and the doctor, summoned again, said again that she must go away. Again the husband was reluctant to leave his work, and the wife insisted that they should stay where they were. Finally, she became so ill that the end appeared at hand. Then the husband called the doctor in and said that he would give up his work and his position and go anywhere. But the physician said it was then too late. However, the professor did give up his position, the family went away, and beyond all expectation the wife recovered. Essentially this story, which can readily be believed, has very much in common with the plot of the *Alcestis*.

XII

THE *MEDEA* OF EURIPIDES

THE *Medea* is certainly the greatest of Euripides' plays. It is one of the most moving dramas in all literature, but not the most enjoyable. An introduction by the grammarian Aristophanes says that it was produced in the archonship of Pythodorus, i.e. 431 B.C., the year in which the Peloponnesian War began: Euphorion was first (i.e. won the first prize in the competition of tragedies), Sophocles was second, and Euripides third with the *Medea, Philoctetes, Dictys,* and the *Harvesters,* the last of these being a satyr-play.

The play presents "a bit of life," human life, although the principal characters are chosen from among the heroes, who were at least something more than men, and although the examples which they furnish of human passions and wickedness are extreme. There is some use of magic in the play; but doubtless this did not seem as incredible to the original audience as it seems to us, and anyway it is an unessential expedient which could easily be replaced by other devices. Briefly the story is of two persons who once fell passionately in love, who then ruthlessly sacrificed everything and everybody else to accomplish their own desires, became involved in a series of crimes, but failed ultimately to achieve permanent success and happiness. Finally, their interests, which had coincided heretofore, became opposed. The man found that by marrying a princess he could obtain a young and beautiful wife, and with her a kingdom: he therefore decided to abandon his former companion. The latter, then, finding means of safety for herself, killed the princess (incidentally, also the princess's father) and her own children. Thus the selfishness of both these persons was directed against others as long as their own interests coincided; but when their own interests were opposed each turned against the other, and treated the other as previously both together had treated everybody else.

The legends on which the play was based are not very old, compared with some. They do not have the appearance of being cult-legends, for they have no apparent religious significance, and they are certainly not allegories of natural phenomena. They are attached to and probably were outgrowths of the Argonaut legend, which reflects the conditions of the eighth, perhaps of the ninth century B.C., when the Greeks were beginning to voyage out to unknown lands as adventurers, traders, or settlers. Jason was the son of Aeson, the king of Iolcus in Thessaly. Pelias, half-brother or some relation of Aeson, usurped the throne. When Jason was grown and demanded his father's kingdom, Pelias agreed to abdicate in his favor if he would bring back the golden fleece, the most cherished possession of Aeetes, the king of Colchis. Jason collected a band of heroes, the greatest heroes of all before the Trojan War, and with them, in the good ship *Argo* which was built for them, sailed to Colchis, somewhere near the farthest shores of the Black Sea. Aeetes promised to give the fleece to Jason if he would yoke the fire-breathing bulls, plow with them a certain field, sow there the dragon's teeth and fight the armed men who would spring up from this miraculous seed, and finally overcome the sleepless dragon which in a strong tower guarded the fleece itself. These tasks were of course impossible for any man. But Medea, Aeetes' daughter, fell in love with Jason, and by her magic enabled him to perform the tasks. So he actually got the fleece, took Medea with him, and escaped. When Medea's brother, Absyrtus, attempted to intercept them, they killed him.

When the *Argo* returned to Iolcus, Medea showed the daughters of Pelias how she could cut an old ram in pieces, boil the pieces in a caldron and bring out a lamb; she said that in the same way she could make Pelias young again. So they cut the old king in pieces and boiled the pieces in the caldron; but no young man came out: Pelias was dead. In consequence of this, Jason and Medea had to leave Iolcus. They took refuge in Corinth, where they were allowed to reside. Perhaps the king of Corinth gave them an allowance on which they could live. But after a while it seemed to the king that it would be a good thing for Jason to desert Medea, marry the king's daughter Glaukē, and become the king's successor. Jason agreed, and the king gave orders that Medea should leave Corinth at once. This story forms the background of the play. There were also legends that when Medea was abandoned by Jason she killed the children whom she had borne to him, and that there was some connection between her and Aegeus, the king of Athens, whom in some way she enabled to beget a son. This was all the legendary material which Euripides had for his drama, the *Medea.*

The play opens with the appearance of a nurse, whose soliloquy shows at once that the stage-building now represents the dwelling of Jason and Medea at Corinth. She alludes to the story of the *Argo,* and says that Jason has repudiated Medea in order to marry the princess Glaukē. A male attendant with the children, apparently two little boys, arrives from somewhere out of doors. He discusses the situation with the nurse and tells her that he has heard that Medea is to be expelled from Corinth immediately. While they are talking the voice of Medea is heard several times from the house, showing her violent rage and desperation. When the "pedagogue" and the children have gone into the house the chorus appears. They are Corinthian women who evidently sympathize with Medea and are hostile to Jason. After a song by the chorus and a musical dialogue between the chorus and the nurse, Medea herself comes out and makes her speech about woman's unhappy lot:

Of all things upon earth that bleed and grow,
A herb most bruised is woman. We must pay
Our store of gold, hoarded for that one day,
To buy us some man's love; and lo, they bring
A master of our flesh!

(GILBERT MURRAY'S TRANSLATION)

Then Creon, the king of Corinth, appears and orders her to leave the city at once. He evidently considers her dangerous, but he is not altogether heartless or impervious to her personal charm or without some recognition that she is being ill treated. She begs him to allow her to remain for one single day, so that she may make some provision for her children, and he at last consents, somewhat reluctantly and obviously against his judgment. This one day allows her to plan and execute her revenge. When he has gone she considers aloud various methods of revenge available to her, and the chorus sings an ode of sympathy and foreboding.

Then Jason appears, apparently from the king's palace, and with Medea engages in a most bitter conversation. Jason tries to excuse his conduct by specious explanations and protests of fair motives: he was striving to obtain a permanent security for them all — for the children and for her, as well as for himself — but she has spoiled everything by her unbridled temper, her unwillingness to assist in his plans, and her foolish, evil speaking against the rulers. She answers him with rage and contempt.

After another choral ode, which adds nothing to the situation, Aegeus appears. He comes from Delphi where he had gone to inquire of the oracle how he may have a son to continue his royal line. The answer he received was not clear, and now he is on his way through Corinth to Troizênē to find a certain Pittheus there and seek enlightenment from him. Thus Medea learns what childlessness means to a man like

Aegeus, and perhaps, as some have supposed, this interview suggested to her that the greatest injury she could inflict on Jason would be to kill his children and the new wife which he proposed to take. But the scene with Aegeus has a much more important significance than this. Medea tells Aegeus that Jason intends to abandon her and marry the Corinthian princess, and that Creon has ordered her to leave the country. Aegeus says that this is a shameful outrage. She begs him to give her his protection and a refuge in Athens: she will provide a remedy for his childlessness — doubtless meaning that she will do this by her magic. Aegeus says that in Creon's country he has no power to protect her, but that if, without his assistance, she can reach the territory of Athens, he will grant her request. She makes Aegeus confirm his promise with an oath. Aegeus swears the oath, and takes his leave. Thus there has been provided for Medea complete security for herself if she can escape from Corinth and reach Athens. She knows how she can do that. So she proceeds at once to make her plans and to carry them out.

She first prepares gifts for the princess, a golden wreath and a robe of such magic power that when the princess puts them on she will die miserably, as will anyone who touches her. Strangely enough she tells the chorus what she means to do: she will kill the princess and then her own children. The women entreat her not to do this, but she is not dissuaded. She sends for Jason, and actually abases herself before him. She apologizes for her former temper and angry words, praises him for his wise forethought, expresses willingness now to do all he wishes. She sends for the children as if she were really reconciled. She is under such strong emotion that her speech is somewhat incoherent and sometimes sarcastic. Jason is fatuous, self-righteous, and pompous. He forgives her for her previous conduct. He even expresses affection for their children, which may be at least partly sincere, and asks if she is not glad of what he is doing. She says that she knows it is best for her to leave Corinth, but begs that the children may be sent with their attendant to carry gifts to Glaukē and ask her to persuade her father to allow the children to stay. Jason consents, though he assures Medea that his influence over Glaukē is such that presents are not necessary. A maid is sent for the deadly gifts, and with them the children and their attendant leave for the royal palace.

The chorus sings another ode. These women now have no more hope for the children's lives; they are beginning to turn against Medea. The attendant brings the children back and tells that the princess has accepted the gifts and that the children will be allowed to stay in Corinth. But Medea is not pleased. In a long speech she says that she cannot endure to be scorned and mocked, as she will be if she gives her children to those who have so abused her. She shows her passionate love for the children and fondles them; but all the while she is obviously trying to steel her heart to take their lives. Finally she sends the children away and follows them into the house. The chorus sings of the sorrows which children bring to a mother.

Presently Medea comes out again and meets a messenger from the palace, who tells her that when the princess put on the poisoned robe she died at once in agony, and that her father, when he touched her, died also. The messenger withdraws, and soon afterwards Medea, who goes back into the house after telling the women that now she is really going to kill the children. After another choral ode, the cries of the children are heard from within. The women start to rescue them, but the door is closed. Then Jason arrives. He knows now that the princess and the king have been killed by Medea's magic gifts, that she is determined to have her revenge and will stick at nothing; he wishes to save the children. The women tell him that the children are already

dead. He orders his men to break down the door. But suddenly Medea is seen on the house top, where a car drawn by
winged dragons awaits her. In the car she has placed the
bodies of her sons. Jason curses her passionately, and she
replies bitterly and taunts him. He says that in killing the
children she has brought pain upon herself. She tells him
that she is glad of this pain if he will laugh no more. Finally
he changes his tone and begs her to give him the children's
bodies to mourn over them. But she refuses, and disappears
in the dragon-car, leaving Jason desolate.

Horrible as it is for a mother to kill her children, such
cases are not unheard of. In the *New York Herald Tribune*
of March 22, 1938, there was the story of a woman, twenty-
five years of age, who while her husband was away from
home smothered to death their two children, a little girl three
years old and a baby boy of five months. This news item
ended with the words: "She blamed family bickering." The
court declared this woman insane. I do not think that Medea
was insane. Doubtless her motives for killing her children
were confused: it is not easy to understand them completely.
But in the arguments by which she drives herself to commit
this act, at least three reasons emerge clearly.

1. She wished to inflict the greatest possible injury on
Jason. He evidently loved his children as much as he could
really love anyone. That is made evident at least in the last
scene. Besides, if she killed these children and the princess
whom he expected to marry, then Jason would probably be
permanently childless, like Aegeus.

2. She was unwilling to leave the children for anyone else
to enjoy. If she could not have them, no one else should.

3. She could not endure to be despised, to be laughed at
as one stripped and cast aside with impunity. This seems to

me the strongest motive of all, and it is manifested especially in lines 797, 807 *ff*., 1049 *f*. and 1361 *f*.

The Aegeus scene seems to me to contain the turning-point of the play. I think it was created by Euripides for the following reasons.

1. Before this scene the audience, even if they really knew the outcome, might still hope that somehow fear of the consequences to herself would deter Medea. This scene removes that hope.

2. Perhaps also the talk with Aegeus did suggest to Medea the form of revenge which she will choose. At least it reveals to the audience one element in this revenge.

3. But chiefly, I think, Medea, in hesitating until she had arranged a refuge for herself, shows that even in her passion she thought it important to provide for her own security, and thus she reveals herself as hard and calculating as well as ruthlessly selfish and cruel. Of course she knew all the while that she could escape from Corinth in the dragon-car at any time.

There is no reason whatever for supposing that, as Sir Gilbert Murray once thought, Medea, because she was a foreigner, was not properly married to Jason. At Iolcus and at Corinth she was accepted as Jason's wife. Nor is there any good reason to assume that she planned to deal with Aegeus's childlessness by bearing children to him herself.

It is significant that in this play neither Medea nor Jason contemplated suicide. Of course the legends did not have it so. But there are dramatic reasons besides. For complete revenge it was necessary that Medea herself should live, lest Jason say: Well, she paid for her revenge anyway. Hence, not alone for her own sake, but for the completeness of her revenge she must remain alive. It was necessary for Jason to live in order that he might suffer more.

Jason and Medea were both thoroughly selfish persons. I think that Euripides, in choosing this subject and in constructing this play, had a purpose besides the ordinary intention of a poet to produce effective drama. I think this purpose was to show that selfish lives bring calamity upon the selfish ones themselves, as a result of their own selfishness, and that among the evil consequences of selfishness to such persons is the deterioration of their own characters: they destroy their own selves.

The most moving part of this most moving drama is the scene in which Medea drives herself to carry out her resolution to kill the children whom she loves.

XIII

THE *IPHIGENIA IN TAURIS* OF EURIPIDES

THE *Iphigenia among the Taurians* is a genuine "tragedy" in the ancient Greek sense. To us it seems a good deal like what we would call a melodrama. It has some moments of high tension, expresses some noble thoughts and feelings, and throughout its whole length arouses in the audience or the reader emotions of sympathy and fear. But then some melodramas have such moments and make such appeal to the emotions also.

The background of the play is furnished by the legends of the House of Atreus, on which the plots of Aeschylus's *Oresteia* were based, in particular the story of the apparent sacrifice of Iphigenia by her father Agamemnon at Aulis to appease the wrath of the goddess Artemis, in order that the Greek host might set out for Troy; and also the story of Orestes who was pursued by the Furies because he killed his mother Clytemnestra. Some material for the plot itself was provided in certain other, less well known, legends. There was one which told that Iphigenia was not really sacrificed by her father, but was rescued at the last moment by the goddess herself, who substituted a hind for the maiden and transported the latter to a far distant land, where she became a priestess of an Artemis worshipped by the barbarians who lived there. Another legend told how, in order that Orestes might be freed from the pursuit of the Furies, the oracle of Apollo at Delphi directed him to bring to Greece from a distant land occupied by barbarians (that is, of course, by a non-Greek people) a statue of the goddess Artemis which had fallen from the sky. Orestes, with his companion Pylades, did so, and was delivered from the Furies. Lastly there were some fairly old traditions connected with the cult of an Artemis "Tauropolos," who was worshipped at Brauron, an ancient town in Attica almost due east from

Athens and near the east coast, and also at Halae on the coast a little north of Brauron, and elsewhere. Apparently this goddess was originally called Iphigenia and, as this name implies, had power over childbirth. Later she was identified with Artemis, doubtless because the latter, being associated with the moon whose phases occupy periods of approximately four weeks, was believed to have some connection with woman's life. Probably she was then called Artemis-Iphigenia. After a while the name Iphigenia was regarded merely as an epithet of Artemis, or as the name of a human person who was associated with the goddess as a priestess and reputed to be a daughter of Agamemnon. It is said that there was a very ancient and primitive statue of this goddess at Brauron or at Halae. The original significance of the epithet *Tauropolos* is uncertain. Some suppose that it implies that this goddess was the patron divinity of cattle herdsmen. But the adjective *ataurōtos* applied to a maiden in Aeschylus's *Agamemnon,* line 245, suggests that the epithet may have had something to do with conception. In any case the epithet itself suggested to the Greeks that there was some connection between this goddess and the Tauroi, a barbarous folk supposed to live somewhere along the shore of the Black Sea, perhaps in the Crimea, and that the archaic statue came originally from them. It was believed that the grave of the priestess Iphigenia was at Brauron. Lines 1458-1461 of the *Iphigenia among the Taurians* suggest a tradition that originally human sacrifices were offered in the cult of the Brauronian Artemis. That is all the known legendary or traditional material which Euripides had for this play.

The play, as we have it now, begins with a declamation sixty-six lines long, by Iphigenia. It is not at all clear from where she comes. She tells, talking apparently to herself, that she is Iphigenia the daughter of Agamemnon, who was supposed to have been sacrificed by her father at Aulis, but was

really saved by Artemis and brought to this land of the barbarous Taurians. She is now serving as the priestess of this
goddess, but not in accordance with the customs of the
Greeks: here she is compelled to participate in the cruel practices of these barbarians who sacrifice to their deity the
strangers captured in their country. Then she tells of a dream
which she has had in the past night, and interprets the dream
as meaning that her brother Orestes, on whom rested all her
hopes of rescue, is dead. Therefore, she says, she has summoned her attendants to "this palace of the goddess" that with
these attendants she may perform funeral rites for her
brother.

This opening speech cannot be understood as a soliloquy—
as if a person, thinking aloud, said to himself: "Let me see!
Just what is the story of my life, beginning with my great-
grandfather?" Nobody really says such things to himself,
except perhaps when he is preparing a story to be told later
to someone else. Nor can it easily be supposed that Iphigenia
here is speaking to some companion who entered the orchestra
with her. There is no reference to such a companion, and no
explanation of how this person came to be there, or how this
person left, for at line 66 Iphigenia seems to enter the temple
alone, and obviously there is no one present when Orestes and
Pylades appear. Most of what this speech contains is related
elsewhere in the play and could have been omitted here. Whatever the author wished the audience to know at the outset
could have been brought out by conversation in an organic
scene, as in Sophocles' *Antigone*. But if there were such a
conversation, it is difficult to imagine who the person addressed by Iphigenia could be. If it were someone who was a
resident of the country, a Taurian or one of the attendants
of the priestess, for example, who might have been ignorant
of Iphigenia's past history, such a person would not have
been told about Iphigenia's present circumstances or the bar-

barous rites in which she was obliged to take part. On the other hand, a stranger would not have been there at all: he or she would already have been sacrificed. There is no reason to suppose, as some have suggested, that only male strangers were sacrificed by the Taurians; it would have seemed, at least to any ancient Greek, far more natural to sacrifice women than men to a goddess, if any women strangers ever arrived on these shores. The Greek women who form the chorus, and whose presence is hard enough to explain anyway, are no exceptions to the Taurian custom; they must have been acquired by the king as slaves, by purchase or in some other way, and given by him to the priestess to serve as her attendants. Probably the best explanation of the speech is the common one, that it was frankly addressed to the audience.

There is just such an opening speech in the extant manuscripts of all Euripides' plays, excepting the *Rhesus,* which probably should not be ascribed to Euripides, the *Cyclops,* which is a satyr-play, and the *Iphigenia at Aulis,* which according to the scholia on Aristophanes (*Frogs,* line 67) was not produced until after Euripides' death, and which certainly appears to have been recast and altered a good deal by others. Even this last mentioned drama contains in lines 49-114 a narrative speech which may have been the original opening. Sixteen plays out of the nineteen preserved under Euripides' name have an introductory speech, averaging fifty-eight lines. In five of these it seems clear that no one was present in the orchestra except the speaker: in the *Alcestis, Hippolytus, Ion* and *Trojan Women* the speaker is a god, in the *Hecuba* a ghost. In the *Helen, Andromache, Phoenissae, Electra,* and *Orestes* there was probably no one besides the speaker. In the *Medea* and *Electra* there were possibly some other persons, perhaps residents of the place or others, not included in the cast. In the *Heracleidae, Suppliants, Heracles* and *Bacchae* there were probably some other persons present. But in no single instance does the speaker seem to be speaking to these persons or to anyone in the orchestra, or to be thinking aloud. One can conclude only that in each case the introductory speech is addressed to the audience.

Whatever artistic value these introductory speeches may have, any speech by a character in the play addressed to the audience rather mars the realism which we expect in the Greek drama. And apparently Athenian audiences were very critical of any lack of realism. Aristotle, in his *Poetics,* c. 17, says that an author should have his scenes as it were before his eyes, in order to avoid anything unsuitable or inconsistent. "This," he says, "is illustrated by what happened to Carcinus : Amphiaraus (evidently a character in one of Carcinus's tragedies) was coming out of a temple, and this fact was overlooked by the poet who did not visualize the scene; but the play was hissed off because the audience was offended."

In the *Lives of the Ten Orators,* which used to be included in the works of Plutarch, VII, sec. 11, it is said that the Athenian Lycurgus, in the second half of the fourth century B.C., secured the passage of a law that copies of the tragedies of Aeschylus, Sophocles, and Euripides should be kept in the public archives, and that at the performances of these plays the clerk of the city should compare the speeches of the actors with the official copy and not permit any alterations in the text. This story, which is plausible enough, suggests that such alterations were already common in Lycurgus's time, and perhaps that the introductory speeches in Euripides' plays were not composed by Euripides himself, but by some actors or editors who may have had no experience in constructing a drama and little appreciation of what would appear plausible to the audience, but had a predilection for long declamations.

Of course, in these plays introductions of some sort were necessary, for otherwise the audience, even if the title of the piece had been announced, would not have known the location, or what the stage-building represented, or who the first speaker was. Commonly in the Greek tragedies the first lines identify the speaker and the location, and give some information about the situation; the later speakers either identify themselves in their first words or are identified by the preceding speaker or the chorus. The introductory speech in the *Iphigenia among the Taurians* contains in lines 42-66 what may be the remains of the original opening. Here Iphigenia says: "What new visions night has brought I will tell to the open air—if there is really any help in that." She then tells her dream and her interpretation of it, and expresses her surprise that her attendants, whom she has summoned to the temple, have not yet arrived. This motivation does not seem very convincing to us; but such devices for bringing before the audience what would naturally have been said or done indoors are common enough in the extant tragedies, and were doubtless made necessary by the fact that the lack of movable scenery and stage mechanisms in the ancient theater made indoor scenes impossible. But this motivation does not apply to the rest of the speech. If Iphigenia had already spoken at some length, the explanation of her reason for telling her dream is not only unnecessary but also inconsistent with what precedes. Only, if lines 42-66 belonged to an original opening, this must have been curtailed and altered somewhat. In the original the speaker must at least have identified himself.

As it stands, however, this introductory speech contains a pertinent and fairly vivid narrative. Much of it recalls Aeschylus's *Oresteia*. In particular one might compare *Iphigenia* lines 10 (and 141), 15, and 27 with *Agamemnon* lines 45, 187 ff., and 235. The statement that Agamemnon had vowed to sacrifice to Artemis the fairest offspring of the year in which Iphigenia was born recalls the story of Jephthah and his daughter in Judges xi. 30-40. Also the story that when Agamemnon was about to sacrifice his daughter at Aulis, a

hind was miraculously substituted for her recalls the story of
Abraham and Isaac in Genesis xxii. 1-19.

After the introductory speech, when Iphigenia has retired,
Orestes and Pylades appear alone, showing by their first
words to each other that they are in a hostile land, engaged
on a most perilous expedition, identifying each other by
name, and indicating that the stage-building is now the temple
of a goddess to whom human sacrifices are offered. Orestes,
in a prayer to Artemis, shows that this is the land of the
Taurians, that the goddess of the temple is Artemis, and that
Apollo has sent him to fetch and bring to the country of the
Athenians the statue of the goddess which fell from heaven,
in order that Orestes may be delivered from the Furies who
pursue him because, by Apollo's command, he killed his
mother. Thus the play is adequately and plausibly introduced,
and the introductory speech by Iphigenia was not strictly
necessary at all. The two young men decide that it is impossible for them to break into the temple and remove the statue
by day, and they retire to hide themselves until night falls.
Then the attendants of the priestess, who compose the chorus,
enter. They tell who they are, and when, after a moment,
Iphigenia comes out, perhaps from the temple, they address
her as the daughter of Agamemnon, thus identifying her.
She says that she is mourning for her brother, believing him
to be dead. Then with her attendants she performs funeral
rites for Orestes in absentia. The chorus laments the evil
fortunes of the House of Atreus, and Iphigenia laments her
own sad life, thereby repeating in other words a good deal of
what was contained in the introductory speech. All this part
of the play is sung, as in a modern opera, and is highly emotional.

Hereupon a Taurian herdsman appears and tells that he
and his companions have just now captured on the shore two
young men. They are Greeks. One of them called the other

Pylades; but the herdsman does not know the other's name or anything more about the captives. At first some of the herdsmen thought these persons were superhuman, but others thought that they were just shipwrecked mariners. While the Taurians hesitated, one of the young men was seized by a sort of madness, fancied that he saw horrible creatures threatening him, and in a frenzy began to attack the herdsmen's cattle. Then the herdsmen rushed upon the young men. The madman fell, foaming at the mouth, his companion protecting him as well as he could. Suddenly the madman seemed to recover his senses, and both he and the other defended themselves valiantly; but finally both were caught. The others took the captives to the king and are now bringing them to the temple. The priestess must prepare to sacrifice these strangers to the goddess as custom requires.

Presently the captives are led in. Iphigenia talks with Orestes, and during her long dialogue with him Pylades does not speak at all. Of course she does not recognize either of them. Both must have been young children when she left home a dozen years or more before; probably she had never even heard of Pylades, although he was her cousin. And of course they do not recognize her: they believed that Iphigenia was long since dead. She asks who they are, these two strangers; but Orestes will not tell her. She asks which of them is called Pylades, and he points to his friend. She asks his own name; but he refuses to give it, saying: "You will sacrifice my body, not my name." He does tell her, however, that his home is Argos. So she begins to ask about the Trojan War and the Greeks who were involved in it. She learns that Troy has fallen. Helen is living with Menelaus again in Sparta; the priestess hates her. The prophet Calchas is reported dead; the priestess is glad of that. Odysseus has not returned; the priestess hopes that he never will return. Achilles is dead. Orestes wonders that the priestess knows so much about

Greece, and asks who she is; but she answers only: "I am from there; I was lost while still a child." Agamemnon too is dead, killed by a woman. Clytemnestra has been killed by her own son. "Did Agamemnon leave any other child in his home?" "Yes, Electra." "Is there any talk of a daughter who was sacrificed?" "Only that she is dead." "Is the son still living?" "He is — miserable, nowhere and everywhere." But this last answer delights Iphigenia, because now she thinks that her dream was false. Orestes says that the oracles of the gods are no less misleading, evidently having in mind the oracles by which he was led to kill his mother and to undertake his present disastrous mission.

Then Iphigenia has an idea. She cannot save both young men, but perhaps she could manage to save one of them. If she can contrive his escape, would the young man with whom she is talking carry a letter to Greece for her? She has had the letter ready for a long time now, waiting for some opportunity to send it. Orestes heartily approves of this plan, but says that he cannot be the one to escape, leaving his friend to die; this expedition was on his own account, he brought his friend into this trouble; the friend must be the messenger and escape while he himself remains to die. The priestess agrees to that and goes off to get the letter.

While she is gone Orestes and Pylades discuss the situation. They wonder who the priestess is. Pylades says that he can not accept her offer of escape for himself and thus desert his friend. At last, however, he is persuaded. The priestess returns with the letter, but, before giving it to Pylades, requires him to swear an oath that he will deliver the letter to her "friends." He takes the oath, and she in turn swears to effect his escape. Then it occurs to Pylades that the letter may be destroyed if his ship is wrecked, or lost in some other way, and the priestess reads the letter aloud so that if it is lost and he is saved he may be able to repeat the message. The letter begins: "Say to Orestes, Agamemnon's son, that she who was slain at Aulis, living still, Iphigenia, sends this message." Orestes asks: "Where is she?" "She is here before you," the priestess replies, "but do not interrupt me. Bring me back to Argos, oh my brother, before I die, from a barbarous land, and deliver me from offering human sacrifices to a goddess!" Thus ingeniously and convincingly it is made known to the two young men that the priestess is Orestes' sister, for the letter is obviously genuine. But to convince the priestess that the young men are her brother and cousin is not so easy. Pylades, of course, hands the letter to Orestes immediately and tells the priestess that thus he keeps the vow he swore. Naturally she hesitates to believe him; naturally she suspects these strangers of pretending that one of them is her brother in order to induce her to try to save them both. But Orestes finally persuades her by describing the embroidery on which she was working when she was taken from home, and by telling of the bridal bath sent to Aulis for her by their mother who supposed that she was to be wedded to Achilles, of the lock of hair which she sent back to their mother when she thought that she was to be sacrificed instead of married, and lastly of the spear of Pelops which was hidden away in Iphigenia's chamber. When she has accepted him as truly her brother, he then identifies Pylades to her. This is by far the best recognition scene in all the extant Greek tragedies, and it was esteemed the best by Aristotle, who had far more ancient plays from which to choose than we have now.

After a good deal of discussion between these three close relatives, Iphigenia devises a plan, counting on the credulity and superstition of the barbarians. She will say that the young men are polluted. They have touched the sacred image, and therefore this has been polluted too. All must be bathed in the sea to purify them before the sacrifice can be performed. Thus they will escape in Orestes' ship. She begs the

other women to keep the secret, and promises that if she is
saved herself she will bring about their safe return to Greece.
Then she and the young men enter the temple.

After a song by the chorus, contrasting the fortune of
those who must remain in captivity with the prospect of
escape for the priestess and her kinsmen, and expressing the
passionate longing of these Greek women for their homes,
Thoas, the king of the Taurians, appears with his attendants,
and meets Iphigenia coming out of the temple with the image
in her arms. It may of course be assumed that the image was
a small wooden statuette like some of the archaic Greek
"xoana." He is surprised and shocked. Addressing her formally as "Daughter of Agamemnon," he asks what she is
doing with the image. She tells him to stand back. He is so
surprised now that he drops all formality, calls her Iphigenia,
and asks what the matter is. She says: "Evil, avaunt!" (The
word she uses means *I spat it off*. It was a common superstition, and still is commonly believed in southern Europe and
the Near East, that spitting averts evil. Doubtless the notion
was commonest among vulgar and uncultured people, and by
this expression Iphigenia lowers herself to Thoas's intellectual level.) Then she adds: "The victims we caught are
unclean." "How do you know," he asks. She tells him that
when the captives approached, the image of its own accord
turned away from them and closed its eyes. On seeing this
she had questioned the young men and had learned that they
had killed their mother. They are polluted. The image has
been polluted too. All must be bathed in the sea, in a deserted
spot, since privacy is necessary for this and for other things
which she has to do. The king trusts her. He says: "Take
them where you will; I have no wish to be a witness of
mysteries." He asks what she wishes him to do. She says:
"Have the strangers bound." — He gives the order. "Have
the strangers brought here . . . covering their heads. Let

guards go with me. Issue a proclamation to all the people to stay indoors and keep out of sight." He sends a man to pass this word around, and says to the priestess: "How you care for the people!" "And for those for whom I should care the most," she replies. "You mean me," says the fatuous king. "Naturally," she says, and adds that he himself must stay behind to purify the temple with a torch (or perhaps with incense or some such thing), and that when the strangers come out, he must hold his cloak before his eyes. "If I seem to be gone too long," she says — he interrupts her, asking how long he is to wait. She ignores this question, and continues: "Be not surprised." He agrees to everything, telling her that she must do all the goddess requires properly, without haste. So the Taurians present in the orchestra leave, excepting the king and the guards detailed to escort the priestess; the king covers his head with his cloak; the prisoners with their heads covered are brought out, and they with the guard and with Iphigenia march off towards the sea. She is carrying the image in her arms and cries out to all to avoid this pollution: "If any ministrant of the temple would remain pure for the service of the gods, or if any think on marriage, or are heavy with child, flee and keep away, lest the taint fall on anyone!" Then the king enters the temple, and the chorus is left alone.

After a song by the chorus, which marks a lapse of time, one of the guards returns in great excitement, calling for the king. The Greek women who compose the chorus, in order to gain time for Iphigenia and the young men to escape, say that the king has left and that the guard must look for him elsewhere. But the man, who now distrusts these Greek women, insists on making sure that the king is not in the temple. Hearing the commotion the king comes out and hears the story: the maid who used to be their priestess here is Iphigenia; one of the strangers is her brother Orestes.

They are now escaping with the holy image. When the party came near the cape, where later it was found that Orestes' ship was hidden, the priestess told the guards to remain at a distance, because she was about to perform secret rites. She herself, taking in her own hands the cord which bound the captives, walked on behind them. That seemed suspicious, but the guards obeyed the priestess's orders. But after a while they went to see what was going on, and found a Greek ship with fifty rowers, oars in place, making ready to start, and on the shore near the ship the two young men freed from their shackles. The guards rushed upon them, caught hold of the ship's cables, and seized the priestess to bring her to the king by force. One of the guards shouted out: "By what right are you trying to steal off with images and priestesses? Who are you?" And one of the young men answered: "I am Orestes, son of Agamemnon, and this is my sister whom I am taking home." Then there was a fight, with fists and feet, for neither the former captives nor the guards were armed. Finally, with the assistance of archers on the ship, the two strangers drove off their assailants, Orestes carried out to the ship his sister, along with the image which fell from heaven, and the ship got under weigh. When the boat reached the open sea, however, it met a strong adverse wind and heavy waves which began to drive it back to the shore again. In vain the priestess prayed to Artemis to save them. In vain the rowers sang and strained. They are about to be stranded. The guard has been sent to call the king to come with cords and nooses, for now Poseidon, lord of the sea, patron of Ilium, will doubtless deliver into the king's hands the son and the treacherous daughter of Agamemnon. It is a long story, and on a modern stage would make an exciting scene or two.

Thoas promptly calls on his people to hurry to the place and capture these impious fugitives if they are driven ashore, and

sends others to launch swift ships to pursue the boat if it
succeeds in getting out to sea. But at that moment the goddess
Athena appears. She bids Thoas to abandon the pursuit, for
it was ordained by the decrees of Apollo that Orestes should
come here and, escaping the wrath of the Furies, should
bring his sister and the image to the country of the Athenians.
"Even now," she says, "Poseidon, for my sake, is giving safe
conduct for this ship, making calm the waves." Then she
speaks to Orestes who, though distant, can hear her voice
because she is a goddess. She tells him to take the image and
his sister to Attica. There at Halae he is to build a temple
and place in it this statue of the goddess whom men shall call
Artemis Tauropolos, in memory of the Taurian land and
of his wanderings. And he shall also establish the custom
that, when the people celebrate the festival of this goddess,
one shall put a knife to the throat of a man and draw blood,
as atonement for the intended sacrifice of Orestes which
was not accomplished. To Iphigenia she says that she shall
be priestess of Artemis at Brauron, and there she shall die
and be buried, and there she shall be honored with offerings
of garments left by those who die in childbirth. She also
charges Thoas to send the Greek maidservants home. This
speech contains a good deal of irrelevant antiquarianism in
the reflection of the legends of Brauron and Halae, which
are mentioned above on page 155 *f.*, and also describes the
very silly derivation of the epithet *Tauropolos* from the
name of the Taurians and the verb *poleō*, to wander; but
such things are not unfamiliar in Euripides' plays.

Thoas says that it is foolish to disobey the commands of
the gods. He will not be angry with Orestes and his sister,
if they have escaped with the image. How is it good to
struggle against the powerful gods? Let them take the image
and go to Athena's land. He will also send the women attendants of the priestess home to blessed Greece, as the

[168]

goddess directs. He will abandon pursuit of the fugitives, according to the good pleasure of the goddess. His speech is somewhat confused and incoherent, but it is natural enough that in the circumstances the king should be a bit confused. What follows, however, is not entirely natural, and suggests that there may be some hidden meaning behind the words. Athena praises the king, apparently for his submissiveness, and then exclaims: "Go, ye winds, and blow Agamemnon's son to Athens, and I will be with you!" Then the chorus, ending the play, sings: "Go, and be happy in the happiness of your deliverance! Oh, holy Pallas Athena, we will do as thou dost command; for very joyful and unexpected are the tidings we have heard!"

There is one very striking thing about this play, which is very hard to explain. After all is over, after Orestes and his good friend Pylades and his sister Iphigenia have overcome all difficulties, have escaped with the statue of the goddess, and are off for home, and when everyone, except perhaps the savage Taurians, is satisfied, then a storm drives the ship back upon the land again and all is lost, until Athena miraculously appears and saves the fugitives by her divine intervention. All this seems perfectly unnecessary. The play was happily finished; now it begins anew.

Is it possible that this last scene was added because, without it, the play was not quite long enough? That is very hard to believe, and anyway, even if this play had ended after line 1378, without the last scene but with the addition of a few lines, which would then have been necessary to conclude the piece and are now omitted, the play would have been longer than five others of Euripides', not counting the *Cyclops,* the *Alcestis,* and the *Heracleidae* which seems to be incomplete.

Was this scene added merely because the Athenian audience liked to see gods in action, especially their own patron goddess Athena? I do not believe that either.

The play was produced certainly after 420 B.C., probably after 414. That would have been after the failure of the Sicilian expedition. Could it have been produced in 410-9, after the Athenians under Alcibiades, who had recently been recalled from exile, had unexpectedly destroyed the Peloponnesian fleet at Cyzicus and temporarily reversed the tide of the war, so that it is said that the Spartans offered to make peace, and the Athenians refused because they then believed that they would be ultimately successful? Or could it have been in 406-5, after the Athenians in desperation had raised one last fleet, compelling all sorts of men, even knights, to go on board, and contrary to all expectation had defeated the Peloponnesian fleet at Arginusae? Could Euripides, or someone else who added this scene to the play, have meant to suggest that the Athenians might win even more victories, might succeed in some more desperate undertakings, but that only their goddess Athena could really save them at the last?

XIV

THE *BACCHAE* OF EURIPIDES

THE *Bacchae* is, at least for modern readers, a mysterious drama. There have been so many attempts to explain it, none of them very convincing or satisfactory. Perhaps the ancient audience understood it. Perhaps there were some undercurrents of thought, now lost to us, which made the poet's meaning clear. There may have been, for example, a strong reaction at that time against the orgies and excesses practised in certain cults, particularly in those much influenced by the religious ideas and customs of "Asia," i.e. the Near East, so that the audience easily recognized this play as a protest against such practices. Perhaps the alarm felt at Athens because the younger Cyrus, with the resources of the Persian government, was helping the Peloponnesian Greeks to win their war against the Athenian Empire, may have had something to do with the conceptions of this play. Cyrus himself was by no means an unmanly person, and certainly could not have suggested to anyone the figure of an effeminate Dionysus. But from 412 B.C. onwards, especially from 407 to 405 B.C., the Persians were a great menace to the Athenians, and this fact may well have caused a feeling of resentment among the latter against all influences from the East. Perhaps we do not easily understand the play only because we do not know what people in its time were thinking and discussing. Or perhaps, when the play was originally produced, much which is now obscure to the reader was made clear to the audience by the performance itself.

A note in the scholia on Aristophanes' *Frogs,* line 67, to which allusion was made above on page 158, states, on the authority of the "Didascaliae," which are the best of sources for such information, that the *Bacchae* formed with the *Iphigenia at Aulis* and the *Alcmeon* a trilogy which was produced after Euripides' death in 407-6 B.C. by his son (or nephew). But that does not indicate when the play was written; the play may have been lying, not wholly finished, among Euripides' papers for some time. It is generally supposed that this was one of its author's latest plays, perhaps his very last. But it shows no failing of his talents due to age or illness. On the contrary, in its dramatic construction, in the beauty of its verses, in the extreme pathos of its last two scenes, it is one of Euripides' best plays.

The early Greeks, even before the times of the Homeric poems, worshiped a god called Dionysus. As said before, this was the god of the springtime. He made the sap to flow, thus producing the new crop of each year, and among all the kinds of sap which flow in plants and trees that most potent juice from which the wine was made. One of the earliest cults of this god was practised at Thebes in Boeotia. There legends grew up which told that this god was born of Semelē, probably a personification of the fruitful earth, and of Zeus, the god of the quickening sunshine and of the clouds, from which comes rain and also lightning. The mother is consumed by the fires of Zeus before her child comes to a natural birth. But the child is saved by Zeus and brought to life by him (i.e. the vine and other plants are brought to maturity by the rain and by the same heat which parches the earth).

Perhaps this god was not always called Dionysus. According to the legends, Zeus gave the child to Hermes, who carried it to the nymphs of Nysa, who nursed and brought it up. One may suppose that there is some connection between the names Nysa and Dio-nysus. But people did not agree as to where Nysa was, if it were a place at all. It was located in Thrace, Macedonia, Thessaly, Euboea, or Boeotia, or on Mt. Parnassus, or on the island of Naxos, or in Caria, Lydia or Cilicia, or in Arabia, Ethiopia, India or Libya (L. Preller, *Griechische Mythologie,* revised by Carl Robert, Vol. I, 1894, p. 663). The fact is that the Greek Dionysus came to be identified with a god, or with various gods, much worshiped in the East as having to do with nature, and fertility, and reproduction, and some features of the orgiastic festivals of these gods were imported by the Greeks from the Orient. Thus arose the legends of the triumphal progress of Dionysus through the whole world. Thus also the worship of the orientalized Dionysus among the Greeks acquired an emotional, ecstatic, sometimes licentious strain, which seemed to many barbaric and pernicious. The god himself acquired womanish traits, and to his more orgiastic cults women especially were devoted.

Among the best known legends about this god was the story of Pentheus, an ancient king of Thebes in Boeotia. Pentheus was the son of Agavē, who was a sister of Semelē and a daughter of Cadmus. He refused to recognize the divinity of Dionysus who through their mothers was his cousin. Consequently Dionysus smote the women of Thebes with madness, and caused them to engage in the wildest orgies. He also induced Pentheus to disguise himself as a woman and to spy upon the frenzied band, which included his own mother. These women caught Pentheus, and in their madness, imagining him to be some wild creature, tore him to pieces with their bare hands. This is the myth on which Euripides based the plot of his *Bacchae*. Ino and Autonoē, the mother of Acteon, both of them reputed sisters of Semelē and Agavē, were also mythological figures, and at least Ino, if not Autonoē, was associated with Dionysus in other legends.

The play opens with the arrival of The Stranger, who makes a long introductory speech. I am not sure that this speech is the introduction composed by Euripides (see above, p. 159); but if it is, there are some strange things about it. First The Stranger says that he is Dionysus, the child of Zeus whom once Semelē bore. Now, changing from the form of a god to the form of a man, he has come to Thebes and sees here the memorial of his mother who was destroyed by a thunderbolt, the ruins of her dwelling still smoldering with the living fire of Zeus. Apparently Semelē's dwelling was not thought to be the palace itself, but as perhaps adjoining the palace. It must have been rather hard for the audience to imagine that after so long a time the fire was still smoldering. Next he describes how in triumph he passed through the lands of Lydians, Phrygians, and Persians, through Bactria and the country of the Medes, through Arabia the blest, and finally through all Asia which lies along the sea, that he might be a divinity (daimon) manifest to men. This is a strange order in which to list the countries visited, but perhaps neither the poet nor the audience knew much about the geography of the East, or perhaps this speech was meant to illustrate the confusion of ideas involved in the legends of Dionysus. Now he has come to Greece, and first of all to Thebes, where his mother's sisters denied that he was born to Zeus. Therefore he has smitten these women and all the womenfolk of Thebes with madness, compelled them to put on the symbols of his orgies, driven them from their homes to a mountain, where now among the trees and rocks they are debauching themselves with the sons of Cadmus. "For this city must learn, although unwilling, that she is uninitiated in my Bacchic rites, and I must defend my mother, Semelē, by showing to men the divinity whom she bore to Zeus." Then he speaks of Pentheus, who has received the kingdom of his grandfather Cadmus, and who is now fighting against the gods in excluding this god from all worship. Therefore, he will reveal his godhead to Pentheus and to all the Thebans, before passing on to other lands. But if the Thebans attempt by force to drag the Bacchae from the mountains, he will make war upon them with his Maenads. It is for these reasons that he has assumed the form of a mortal man. Lastly, he addresses the group of women who constitute the chorus.

They are Asiatics, and have followed him from Lydia through all his travels. He bids them take their Phrygian tambourines, invented by Mother Rhea and himself, and beat them about the palace of Pentheus here, that all the city of Cadmus may see. Then he withdraws.

The speech is filled throughout with the attempt to demonstrate the divinity of the child of a human mother.

The chorus may have entered with The Stranger, or it may have entered first towards the end of his speech. When he has left them, these Asiatic women sing a wild, extravagant song in praise of Dionysus and his orgiastic worship. The song is full of allusions to the East — Asia, Mt. Tmolus, the Phrygian mountains, Lydia and the river Pactōlus — to oriental divinities such as Cybelē and Rhea, and to semi-divine figures such as the Curetes and Corybantes. It contains fantastic passages such as these: "Blest is the happy man who, knowing the mysteries of the gods, hallows his life and consecrates his spirit on the mountains, keeping the Bacchic festivals with holy rites and duly celebrating the orgies of the Great Mother, Cybelē, and who, waving aloft the thyrsus and wreathed with ivy, serves Dionysus. Go ye Bacchae! Go ye Bacchae! Bring Bromius the god, child of a god, down from the Phrygian mountains to the wide ways of Greece, Dionysus the uproarious (bromius)! Oh Thebes, nurse of Semelē, put on the ivy crown! Bloom, bloom with verdant fair-berried smilax, and join the Bacchic revels, with branches of oak or fir! Deck your dress of dappled fawn-skins with twisted locks of glistening wool! Make you holy amid the insolent wands! Soon will the whole earth dance, when Bromius leads his bands from mount to mount where the crowd of womenfolk abides, driven in frenzy from looms and shuttles by Dionysus. . . . Lovely upon the mountains whoever of the coursing revelers falls to the ground, wearing the holy dress of fawn-skins, hunting the blood of goats slain and the delight of eating raw flesh, rushing to the mountains Phrygian, Lydian, when Bromius leads!" This song shows what these Asiatic women thought about the Greek-Asiatic Dionysus and his orgies.

I think that in the next scene, in which Teiresias talks with Cadmus and later Pentheus talks with them both, a clue may be found to the understanding of this play. Teiresias, the aged seer, appears before the palace, to call for his still older friend Cadmus, "who came from Sidon and built the towers of Thebes." He asks someone to announce his presence. Cadmus knows the things about which he has come. These two very old men have agreed together to carry wands, to wear the fawn-skins, and to crown their heads with ivy. Cadmus comes out before the servant can summon him: he was ready and waiting for the call, and recognized his friend's voice. He is dressed in the costume of the god (i.e. of the god's devotees). "As far as we are able," he says, "we must magnify him who is my daughter's son, Dionysus, who has appeared to men a god." He asks: "Where are we to dance?" He says: "Lead me — for I would never weary, night or day, of beating the earth with my thyrsus: in delight we have forgotten that we are old." Teiresias replies: "Then we are alike, for I too am young again, I too will attempt the dancing." Cadmus, however, suggests that perhaps they had better have a carriage to get to the mountain. Teiresias says this would be assuming more dignity than the god (who goes on foot). "Well," says Cadmus, "old as I am, I will lead you, an old man, like a child." "The god," says Teiresias, "will conduct us thither without toil." "Will we be the only ones of the city to dance for Bacchus?" asks Cadmus. "Yes," Teiresias answers, "for we alone are wise, the rest are foolish." "Hold my hand," says Cadmus — "I, being mortal, do not despise the gods." Teiresias replies: "We do not apply reason to the gods. The traditions of our fathers, old as time, no argument refutes." — This is not very logical, because Cadmus has just said that Dionysus is his grandson. Perhaps the prophet means merely that reason and religion have little to do with each other. "Some will say that I disgrace my age, in going to dance with my head crowned with ivy: the god makes no distinction of age."

Then the young Pentheus arrives. He has been absent from the country and has just returned. He has heard of strange evil-doings in the city. The women have left their homes, making pretext of Bacchic rites, and on the wooded mountains they are honoring with dances the new-brought deity, Dionysus, whoever he is. The bands of revelers have with them bowls full of wine, and some are indulging their passions with males, pretending that they are votaries, like Maenads, but they are thinking more of Aphrodite (love) than of Bacchus. "Those, whom I have caught, are imprisoned; those still free I will hunt out of the mountains — Ino, and my mother Agavē, and Acteon's mother Autonoē. — I will soon put a stop to this Bacchic iniquity!" says Pentheus. "They tell me that a stranger has come, a trickster and enchanter from Lydia, with fragrant golden curls, face flushed, and in his eyes the charms of Aphrodite. Day and night he consorts with maidens, teaching them mystic rites. If I catch him, I will stop his thyrsus-beating and his waving his locks of hair!" At this he catches sight of the two old men, the diviner in dappled fawn-skin, the other playing the Bacchant with a wand. "Very laughable," say Pentheus. He is ashamed to see that their age has no sense. He begs his grandfather to throw away the ivy and the thyrsus. But to Teiresias the young king speaks angrily: "This is your persuasion," he says. "You wish, by bringing in to men this new deity, to have profit from divinations and sacrifices. If your hoary age did not protect you, you would be sitting bound among the Bacchae, for introducing immoral rites. For where there is gladness of the grape at women's feasts, there is no longer soundness in the celebrations." The chorus protests briefly against Pentheus's blasphemy and his disrespect for Cadmus and his own family. But Teiresias makes a long and pompous address. He speaks like a suave and casuistical cleric. He rebukes the young man for his callow glibness. He says that this new divinity whom Pentheus mocks will have in Greece such power as he himself could not describe. Demeter nour- ishes mortals with solid food. Dionysus brought to men wine, which releases them from suffering, giving them sleep and forgetfulness of daily ills. Himself a god, he is poured out in libation to the gods, so that thus mankind is blest. (Such confusion of the gift with the giver is not unfamiliar to us in religious literature.) Then, in a passage twelve lines long which some consider spurious, he rationalizes the myth of Dionysus's birth and upbringing. After this he defends the madness which this god bestows. Bacchic frenzy and dementia are fraught with prophecy, when the god in power enters the body. In war also he strikes armies with terror before ever the spear is touched: this also is madness from Dionysus. "And you will yet see him on the rocks of Delphi leaping with torches, brandishing and shaking the Bacchic wand, grown great throughout Greece," i.e. Greece will soon be con- verted. "Believe me, Pentheus," he says. "Think not that human might prevails nor, if you think it and if your reason is distraught, imagine that you are wise. Receive the god into the land! Make libation to him, join the Bacchic rout, crown your head!" He defends the orgies. Dionysus will not compel women to restrain their passions. That lies in their nature. Even in the Bacchic revels she who is self-controlled will not be corrupted. "Therefore I and Cadmus, whom you laugh at, will crown our heads with ivy and will join the dance, a hoary pair — still we must dance. And I will not fight against the gods because of your words."

Cadmus is not so disputatious; he speaks as one of the family: "My boy, Teiresias has given you good advice. Abide with us! Do not flout these ways (customs or practices)! Even if this is not a god, in your opinion, say that he is! Tell a noble lie, in order that men may believe that Semelē bore a god, and that all our family may have honor! Remember the wretched fate of Acteon [Pentheus's cousin] who was torn in pieces by his own savage hounds because he boasted that he was a better hunter than Artemis!"

Pentheus tells his grandfather not to touch him. He says: "Go, join the revels, but contaminate me not with your folly! However, I will punish this instigator of your foolishness." Then he sends a man to destroy the shrine where Teiresias practises his divination, and to throw all the diviner's properties to the winds. He sends others to catch the effeminate stranger who brings a new disease to women and corrupts their chastity. Teiresias says: "Wretched man, you do not know what you are saying; you are crazy now and you were witless before. Let us go, Cadmus, and beseech the god to spare this savage man and the city! Follow me, and try to support me as I support you! It were disgraceful for two old men to fall down. Still, let that pass: we must serve the Bacchic god, the son of Zeus!"

So these two old men totter away, dressed as Bacchants, supporting each other. The prophet has made a long theological argument in favor of this strange religion, and has asserted that its rites do no harm; if the women are continent naturally they will not be injured. The other, once a ruling monarch, urges the present king to tell a pious falsehood, and say that this Dionysus is a god, even if he does not believe it, for then they will have the credit of having a god in the family, and Pentheus himself will escape mischance. Thus both are sophistical, pragmatic, disingenuous, and both are made to appear ridiculous. Representatives of an older generation, they are feeble advocates of orgiastic worship.

The chorus sings again, in much the same strain as before. These Asiatic women protest against the insolence of Pentheus. They extol the festivals of their god, the dances, the music, the joy of wine to gods and men. "It is foolish," they say, "for men not to think men's thoughts. Life is short!" They express their longing to come at last "to Cyprus, Aphrodite's isle, where dwell the Loves beguiling the hearts of men, or to the land which the streams of a barbarous river with its hundred mouths makes fertile without showers, or to Pieria the Muses' home, the sacred slopes of Olympus. . . . Thither bring us, Oh Bromius, Bromius, Leader of Bacchants, Spirit to whom our shouts resound! There are the Graces, there Desire, there it is meet for the Bacchae to hold their revels. . . . This spirit, the child of Zeus, rejoices in festivals. — He gave to rich and poor alike the carefree delight of wine. . . . He hates those who care not for these things, or do not wish to live a joyful life by day and night. It is wisdom to keep one's mind and heart free from meddlesome men. Whatsoever the humbler crowd approves and practises, that we accept." It does not seem to me that this play represents, as some have thought, "the conflict between a flippant scepticism" and "religious faith."

Throughout the rest of the play there is frequent mention of miracles which seem to occur through the power of this god. But these miracles are described by various persons and are not seen by the audience. Of course it would have been difficult, if not impossible, to present miracles visibly in the ancient theater. But perhaps the audience was expected to understand that these things did not really happen, and were imagined or deliberately invented by those who tell about them. For example, the chorus in lines 591 *ff.* bids all to

see the architraves (apparently of the palace) crumbling, and
the fire burning around the tomb of Semelē. When The
Stranger comes out of the palace he says that Bacchus shook
the building and kindled fire on the tomb. In his first speech
he had spoken of the fire still burning there. A few lines
further on, he says that the god dashed the buildings to the
ground, and that the whole structure lies in ruins. Yet later
in the play the palace seems to be intact, and people go into
and come out of it normally. Also, in line 509 Pentheus had
ordered his attendants to confine the captive in the stables.
But in lines 618 *ff.* The Stranger says that the king found
a bull in the stalls where he was imprisoning his captive,
having brought the prisoner there apparently by himself
without the assistance of his attendants, and that the king,
supposing that the bull was the captive, bound the bull with
cords, then, thinking the palace was on fire, called to his
servants to bring water, then, imagining that the prisoner
had escaped, got his sword and tried to kill The Stranger,
but found instead a phantom created by the god and stabbed
the empty air. The reader gets the impression that after
the arrival of this Dionysus everyone in Thebes became crazy.
But the poet obviously intended that the death of Pentheus,
torn limb from limb by his mother and her sisters and other
Bacchants, should be considered real, for convincing evidence
is presented before the play ends that Pentheus was actually
killed in this way. In the play those who participated in this
orgiastic worship really did become temporarily insane, with
a most horrible result.

After the choral ode last mentioned, the king's men bring
in The Stranger, bound. Evidently all believe him to be a
man. The leader of the guards says that the captive made no
resistance, but laughed and told his captors to bind him and
lead him off, so that the leader was impressed and apologized

for the arrest on the ground that he was acting on the king's orders. The guard also says that the captured Bacchæ have escaped: the fetters fell from their feet and keys without human hands opened the doors. Pentheus questions The Stranger; but the latter answers each question evasively and ironically. He does say, however, that he has come from Lydia, and that Dionysus the son of Zeus has brought him here. Pentheus, finally exasperated, orders his men to confine the prisoner in the dark stables. The Stranger is led away, and the king retires into the palace.

Left alone, the chorus sings again. Apparently even these Asiatic women believe that The Stranger is human, one of their fellow-Bacchants, and that the god himself is at some unknown place. They deplore that Thebes, which once received the child of Zeus, now does not welcome his ivy-crowned revelers. They protest against the savage impiety of Pentheus, and call upon the god to restrain the king. They express confidence that the god will come, with his Bacchic revels, and will lead his dancing Maenads over the intervening streams. Then a voice is heard, announcing that the speaker is the son of Semelē and of Zeus. After some conversation between the unseen god and the women, who do not seem even yet to identify the god with their captured leader, The Stranger comes out. He reproves his followers for their anxiety. He tells them about the madness of Pentheus and the miraculous occurrences mentioned two paragraphs above. When he has finished, the king comes out in great excitement, exclaiming that he has been treated outrageously, and that his prisoner has escaped. Catching sight of The Stranger, he demands to know how this person presumes to be there before the palace. The Stranger sternly tells him to stop where he is, and to restrain his anger. While they are speaking, a Theban herdsman appears and tells

what he has seen on the mountain. He and others were driv-
ing their cattle over the hillsides when they saw three bands
of women, of whom Autonoē, Agavē and Ino respectively
were the leaders. The women lay asleep upon the ground
relaxed, but preserving all due modesty — not, as the king
thinks, drunk with wine and music of the flute, and seeking
to gratify their lust in the deserted woods. When the king's
mother heard the lowing of the cattle she wakened the others,
who rose up, a wondrous sight of decorous beauty, women
young and old and maidens still unwed. They let their hair
stream over their shoulders, and girt their fawn-skins about
them, fastening the dappled hides with girdles of snakes
which licked their cheeks. Some held in their arms the young
of gazelles or wolves, and those who had babes at home
suckled these wild creatures. They placed on their heads
crowns of ivy or oak or smilax. One struck a thyrsus into
the rock, and out gushed a stream of water. Another thrust
her wand into the earth, and the god sent forth for her a
spring of wine. Those who wanted milk had only to scrape
the earth with the tips of their fingers; from the ivy-wreathed
wands sweet honey dripped. If the king had been there, this
herdsman says, he would have sought in prayer the god whom
he now repudiates. One of the herdsmen who was familiar
with the city and knew the talk there suggested that to please
the king they should catch Agavē and stop these rites. But
when they attempted to do so, they were attacked by the
women and fled. Then the women attacked the cattle with
their bare hands. Young cows and heifers were dismembered,
ribs and hoofs were thrown about, dripping blood. Even
fierce bulls were dragged to the ground by many maidens'
hands, their flesh torn in pieces quicker than eye could wink.
Now these women sweep over the plains, like enemies swoop-
ing on everything, scattering everything. They snatched chil-

dren from their homes. Whatever they placed on their shoulders stayed there unheld, nor fell to the ground — even bronze or iron. They bore fire on their hair, and were not burned. When some, harried by the Bacchae, rushed to arms, their weapons drew no blood, but the women with their wands wounded the men and put them to flight, not without someone of the gods. "Oh Master, receive this spirit, whoever he is, into our city!"

This whole account is most extravagant. The speaker himself and the king appear to believe it. No one can be sure whether the audience was expected to believe it or to understand that the herdsmen, like everyone else in Thebes, were now insane. It seems to me that the audience has been prepared for such an understanding by the words of The Stranger when he came out of the palace. He said that the god had kindled fire on the tomb of Semelē, and that the palace had crumbled to the ground. The intention of the author might be clear to us if we knew whether the tomb was visible to the audience, and whether it could be supposed that only parts of the palace fell while the front remained intact. Certainly, however, The Stranger says to the chorus that the god has now kindled fire on the tomb, although previously he had said that the fire was already burning there, and he certainly speaks as if the whole palace were destroyed, though the audience can see that this is not true.

After the herdsman's long speech, the king calls out his men-at-arms, to march against the Bacchae. "Nay, but this passes all bounds," he says, "if we are to suffer what we are suffering from women." The Stranger quietly but sternly warns him not to bear arms against a god, not to kick against the pricks: he offers to bring the women to the king without arms. The king calls for his weapons. Then The Stranger asks him if he would like to see for himself the women on the mountains. The king says that he would like to see them in their drunkenness. The Stranger tells him that then he must disguise himself as a woman and a Bacchant. The gradual ascendancy of The Stranger over the mind of Pentheus is very skilfully exhibited. Finally Pentheus agrees to all that The Stranger suggests, and both enter the palace to arrange the disguise.

Left alone the chorus sings a rather enigmatic ode. Twice they say: "What is wisdom, what fairer guerdon from the gods among mortals than to hold one's hand in mastery over the heads of one's enemies? Whatever is fair is dear alway!" "One ought not," they say, "to know more than customs and practices. . . . It is easy to believe that whatever is of supernatural origin, and in the long time is customary and natural, has power."

The Stranger and the king come out again, talking about the latter's appearance. Pentheus is now entirely mad. He says: "I think I see two suns, two Thebes, and you, a bull, seem to go before us with horns upon your head. But perhaps you were once a beast. Certainly you look like a bull." They discuss the king's looks and his dress. Is his hair right? Does his skirt hang straight? The Stranger helps him to complete his dressing, and presently both leave, apparently for the mountain. The chorus sings another wild song, anticipating that Pentheus will be killed by his mother who, though she recognizes him as son of Echion, thinks him born of no human mother, but of some lioness or gorgon or some such thing. The song shows the ideas of a pure and holy life, controlled and subject to the gods, strangely confused with unreasoning superstition and with a savage brutality. Soon a man appears, who had attended the king and The Stranger. He tells the chorus that Pentheus is dead. The women openly rejoice and, replying to the man's indignant protest, say that they are foreigners expressing their feelings in barbarous strains. Then the attendant tells the story. When they came to the mountain the king complained that he could not see the women, whereupon The Stranger bent a fir tree to the ground, and when the king was seated in its branches let the tree slowly up again, so that the king became immediately conspicuous to all the raving Bacchae. These soon crowded around and, when they could not hit the king with stones or with the wands which they threw at him, they pulled the tree down with their hands. Pentheus, now thoroughly frightened, snatched off his headdress, and begged his mother to recognize him and spare his life. But she, foaming at the mouth, with rolling eyeballs, crazed, with her two sisters and the other frenzied women, tore her son limb from limb.

The women of the chorus exult at this account. They say: "A noble deed, to embrace a son with a hand that drips with blood!" But before they can say more Agavē appears, holding in her hands her son's bleeding head, which she is bringing home as a trophy, in the belief that it is the head of some wild animal. This sight is too horrible even for these barbarian women: they appear to be really shocked.

Presently Cadmus returns alone. He went with Teiresias to join the Bacchic orgies on the mountain; but he is now completely sobered. He knows what has happened, and is bringing back all the parts of Pentheus's body which he could find. He sees Agavē with Pentheus's head, and realizes that she is still violently insane. Pathetically, but with a touch of his former sordidness remaining, he exclaims: "How justly the god has punished us, but too severely! Bromius, our lord, has destroyed us — though he is of our family!" He tells his daughter to look up to the sky, then talks to her, reminding her of the past, until she comes to her senses and realizes that it is her son's head which she is holding in her hands. She asks her father finally what part Pentheus had in her

folly, and Cadmus replies: "He was like you, not reverencing
the god: therefore he has involved us all in one ruin, you and
himself and me." Certainly that is not wholly true, for she,
quite independently of Pentheus, had first denied this god's
divinity and then participated in the orgies, while Cadmus,
in spite of Pentheus's ridicule and pleading, had taken part
in the Bacchic rites. Cadmus is evidently not very intelligent,
and he is bewildered; but he is pitiable and very human: he
wants to put the blame on some one other than his daughter
or himself.

Then Dionysus himself appears. Only a part of his speech
is here: the rest has been lost, or perhaps was never written,
for evidently the play was not completely finished by Euripides. What remains of this speech contains an obscure and
jumbled prophecy of the future in store for Cadmus and
his wife Harmonia, doubtless based on legends reflected in
the *Etymologicum Magnum* and in Herodotus IX, c. 42
and 43. But at the end are these lines: "This I say, I Dionysus,
not born of a mortal father but of Zeus. If ye had known
wisdom, when ye would not, ye would have had the son of
Zeus as your ally, and ye would have been happy."

I think that Euripides intended that his audience should
understand that this being who now appears is the real
Dionysus, and that The Stranger embodies a different conception of the god, imported from abroad. Pentheus is
punished because he would not acknowledge either conception. Agavē likewise denied the true god, and was compelled
to join in the worship of the other. Cadmus suffered because,
of his own free will, he chose to serve this other deity. The
orgiastic worship of Dionysus was repugnant to enlightened
Greeks. It had its roots in the superstition and emotional
excitability of the common people, especially among the

women. It might be defended by a dogmatism like that of Teiresias; it might be supported by the hypocrisy of those who, like Cadmus, maintained religious beliefs which seemed to imply a divine sanction for their own waning prestige. But it brought upon such worshipers madness and destruction.

INDEX

INDEX

Absyrtus, 144
Admetus, 131*ff*.
Aegeus, 146*f*.
Aegisthus, 29*ff*., 43*ff*.
Agamemnon, 29*ff*., 63-5
Agavē, 175, 185, 188*f*.
Alcestis, 133*ff*.
Antigonē, 75*ff*., 90
Apollo, 33, 55*ff*., 132
Areopagus, 53
Argo, 144
Artemis, statue of, 155*ff*.
Athena, 51*ff*., 168-70
Autonoē, 175-85

Bacchae, 176, 177, 182, 184, 186
Bacchants, 182, 183, 184
Bacchus, 178, 183
bow, of Heracles, 117, 120, 122, 124-6
Brauron, legends of, 155, 156, 158
Bromius, 177, 178, 182
Browning, Robert, 134
Busse, Bruno, 92

Cadmus, 178*ff*.
Cassandra, 32*f*., 37-9
catharsis, 6
chance, 112
changes of scene, 11, 46*f*., 55-7
Chrysippus, 91
Chthonic deities, 98*f*.
Clytemnestra, 29*ff*., 43*ff*., 65*f*.
comedy, 8*f*.
court, 51*ff*., 68
Creon, 75*ff*., 104*ff*., 146, 148

Death, 132
Dionysus, 3-7, 100, 173*ff*.

Earth-Gods, 98*f*.
Electra, 43*ff*.
Epaphos, 16, 23
Erinyes, 51*ff*., 68
Eumenides, 51, 57

Euripides, 131*f*.
Eurydicē, 75, 79, 85

fate, 112
fear, 6
fire-post, 30*f*., 35*f*.
Furies, 46, 48, 51*ff*., 155, 161*f*.

ghost, 52, 56
Glaukē, 145, 148
God, 61*ff*., 70*f*.
gods, 15*ff*., 52, 54, 69, 168, 170, 176-87

Haemon, 75*ff*.
Halae, legends of, 156, 168
Heracles, 125-7, 134*ff*.

Ino, 175, 185
Io, 15*ff*.
Iocasta, 89, 90, 105*ff*.
Iphigenia, 29, 36, 39, 65, 155*ff*.

Jason, 144*ff*.
Jebb, R. C., 84, 94, 117
justice, 52*ff*.

kindred blood, 33, 46, 52*f*., 67, 69, 110
komos, 8

Laïus, 89, 90, 91, 99, 104*ff*.
legality, 68
letter, Iphigenia's, 163*f*.
love, 85

Maenads, 176, 184
Matthews, Brander, 11*f*.
Medea, 144*ff*.
Meropē, 89, 99, 106
Murray, Gilbert, 150

Neoptolemus, 117*ff*.
Norwood, Gilbert, 131*f*.
Nysa, 174

[193]